MARCO 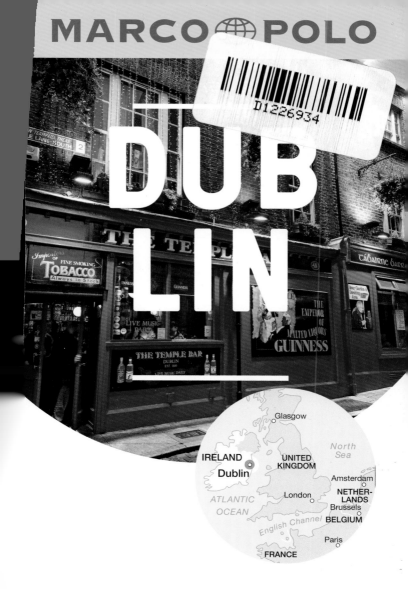 POLO

DUB LIN

D1226934

Glasgow

IRELAND · Dublin · UNITED KINGDOM · North Sea · Amsterdam · NETHER-LANDS · London · Brussels · BELGIUM · ATLANTIC OCEAN · English Channel · Paris · FRANCE

www.marco-polo.com

FREE!

THE TOURING APP

shows you the way...
including routes and offline maps!

GET MORE OUT OF YOUR MARCO POLO GUIDE

IT'S AS SIMPLE AS THIS

1 go.marco-polo.com/dbl

2 download and discover

GO!

WORKS OFFLINE!

SYMBOLS

INSIDER TIP	Insider Tip
★	Highlight
●●●●	Best of ...
ᴬᵢᴸ	Scenic view
☯	Responsible travel: for fair trade and ecological aspects

(*)   Telephone numbers
       that are not toll-free

PRICE CATEGORIES HOTELS

Expensive	over 150 euros
Moderate	100–150 euros
Budget	under 100 euros

The prices are for two people
per night in a double room,
including breakfast

**PRICE CATEGORIES
RESTAURANTS**

Expensive	over 35 euros
Moderate	25–35 euros
Budget	under 25 euros

The prices are for a three-
course dinner without
drinks

CONTENTS

DID YOU KNOW?
Irish roughnecks → p. 22
Time to chill → p. 37
Fit in the city → p. 45
Favourite eateries → p. 58
Local specialities → p. 60
For bookworms &
film buffs → p. 68
More than a good
night's sleep → p. 82
National holidays → p. 105
Budgeting → p. 111
Weather → p. 112

MAPS IN THE GUIDEBOOK
(116 A1) Page numbers and coordinates refer to the street atlas
Map of surrounding area on p. 124/125
(0) Site/address located off the map. Coordinates are also given for places that are not marked on the street atlas

(⌕ A–B 2–3) refers to the removable pull-out map

INSIDE FRONT COVER:
The best highlights

INSIDE BACK COVER:
Public transportation map and map of Temple Bar

The best MARCO POLO Insider Tips

Our top 15 Insider Tips

INSIDER TIP **Dining with Jesus**
Dublin's answer to Leonardo da Vinci: *Dublin's Last Supper* by John Byrnes is on a wall in the Italian Quarter and can be admired day and night free of charge → p. 43

INSIDER TIP **Satisfy your fashion desires**
You can't afford top international designers like Galliano and company? No problem – hire your dream designer outfit from *Covet – The Borrowers Boudoir* → p. 66

INSIDER TIP **Pizza bus and flea market**
A pub of many faces. By day *The Bernard Shaw* is an Italian restaurant, come evening it transforms into a pub serving craft beer, and pizza from a big blue bus in the beer garden, which also hosts a flea market at the weekend → p. 74

INSIDER TIP **Ease up on the credit card**
A great way to save money is to take advantage of some of Dublin's excellent pre-theatre *set menus* → p. 52

INSIDER TIP **The expert's choice**
Museum curators display and discuss their favourite pieces in the *Curator's Room* at the National Museum – Decorative Arts → p. 45

INSIDER TIP **From grave robbers to national heroes**
The *Glasnevin Museum* at the huge cemetery of the same name reveals the secrets of Dublin's 'City of the Dead' → p. 49

INSIDER TIP **Medicinal cocoa**
The founders of this shop at the turn of the 1900s swore by the healing powers of cocoa. These days, *Chelsea Drugstore* serves cocktails and small dishes → p. 71

INSIDER TIP **Creepy catacombs**
This encounter will haunt you: the corpses in the catacombs of *St Michan's Church* have hardly decomposed, despite being hundreds of years old → p. 46

INSIDER TIP The Backroom

There is no secret gambling in The Backroom at Cobblestone – as one might suspect from looking at the name – instead it plays host to famous and up-and-coming *live bands* → p. 74

INSIDER TIP Getting to know the city, bite by bite

On the *Dublin Tasting Trail* you can do some unusual sightseeing when you visit local fresh markets, fishmongers and cheese specialists with plenty delicious food to taste along the way – you will not go hungry on this tour → p. 113

INSIDER TIP Fine ingredients for a picnic

Fashion above, food below: at the *Avocas Food Hall* they have both, beautiful clothing and some extremely delicious goodies on offer. Freshly baked bread, Irish cheese and tasty pies, all perfect for a marvellous picnic on St Stephen's Green just around the corner → p. 65

INSIDER TIP Where Irish roughnecks meet

A live hurling match or a rowdy Gaelic football game at *Croke Park* will certainly be an experience to remember (photo left). Both sports are so quick, you won't have time to get bored → p. 22

INSIDER TIP Sleepless in Dublin

At *Avalon House* you save money while you sleep. Prices from just 10 euros a night including breakfast are very hard to beat → p. 85

INSIDER TIP A mecca for hipsters

The café *The Fumbally* and its fantastic vegetarian food was a mecca for hipsters before the word was even invented. Dogs and musicians welcome → p. 55

INSIDER TIP Bus ride with panoramic views

For a splendid ocean view take the *bus route 31 B* along the coast to the fishing village of Howth (photo below) → p. 51

BEST OF...

FOR FREE

● *Wide view across the city*
The view from *Howth Head* over the Dublin Bay, the mountains and many other parts of the city is free and peaceful. The short ascent isn't too much effort, provided you leave your high heels in your suitcase. It begins behind the Deer Park Hotel → p. 51

● *On the trail of the rock legends*
Dublin's music scene has produced any number of other famous rock musicians besides U2. The *Rock 'n' Stroll Trail* lets you follow in their tracks for free. The brochure and podcast are available on the Internet at no extra charge: download, print and off you go → p. 113

● *An ecologically friendly option*
If your feet hurt from all the sightseeing, then why not let the comfortable and eco-friendly *Ecocab* take you anywhere within Dublin's city centre. The rickshaw-like tricycles are a free service, thanks to corporate sponsorship (photo) → p. 112

● *A long night of Dublin culture*
Dublin has followed the same trend as other European capitals and holds a *Culture Night* every September. The entire city joins in with music, art, readings, and workshops until dawn, museums, theatres, pubs... and best of all is that everything is for free → p. 105

● *Celtic gold*
Despite the economic crisis, the entrance to state museums is still free. Visit the *National Museum* and admire the precious collection with Viking-era exhibits and a gold collection from the prosperous days of the Celtic tribes → p. 32

● *Live music at the pub*
The cost of tickets for live concerts can quickly dent your wallet but that is not the case in Dublin. There are still pubs here where you can enjoy live Irish music for free. Good venues are *The Brazen Head* and *Hughes' Bar* → p. 73, 74

●●●● Dots in guidebook refer to 'Best of...' tips

● *Dublin's poets and the thirst*
If you would like to follow in the footsteps of poets,
you need not worry about getting thirsty on the
way. On the *Literary Pub Crawl*, actors lead you
from pub to pub and as they go along they
recite verses, sing ballads, act out melodra-
mas and talk about the authors' works
→ p. 113

● *Georgian style Merrion Square*
The brightly coloured doors of *Merrion
Square*, built in the Georgian style, will
make quite an impression on you. In the
middle of the park there is a collection of
historical street lamps and a few sculptures,
one of Oscar Wilde, who lived at no. 1 between
1855 and 1876 → p. 31

● *The rich and famous*
If you want to keep an eye out for celebrities, the best place to go is
the *Horseshoe Bar* at the Shelbourne Hotel. This is the place to see and
be seen and the hotel and its bar are a Dublin institution – quite a few
scandals have played out here → p. 81

● *Favourite number game*
Nowhere is Ireland more Irish than at bingo (photo), played most evenings in community halls and at the *National Stadium*. Heads are down
and faces screwed up in concentration until someone calls 'check' – is
it a full house? Next time it could be you!
→ p. 72

● *The heart of old Dublin*
The district known as *The Liberties* got its name during the period when
it was a customs-free zone. Bargain hunters trawl the small shops and
antique stores on Thomas Street and Meath Street. The Guinness Brewery is also located in The Liberties → p. 47

● *Train trip along the coast*
The Irish Sea is always in sight: the *DART* (Dublin Area Rapid Transport)
will take you once around Dublin Bay. The commuter train goes from
Howth and Malahide in the north of Dublin along the coast up to
Greystones in county Wicklow
→ p. 50, 111

ONLY IN

BEST OF...

● *For a pint*
Mulligan's pub – which dates back to 1732 – has been renovated with great care so that you can still drink your beer in an authentic and cosy atmosphere → p. 75

● *Grown under glass*
The original Victorian greenhouses in Dublin's *Botanical Gardens* are exceptional. Take a stroll between the palms and orchids under the remarkable curvilinear glass ceiling and shelter from the rain → p. 50

● *Behind the prison gates*
The *Kilmainham Gaol* is Ireland's Bastille (photo). Walking through the dark building gives you a crash course in Irish history: from 1796 to 1924, the prison was full of Irish rebels who fought against the British occupation → p. 50

● *Eat from the packet*
Visit Ireland's most famous chipper: fish and chips by *Leo Burdock*. It has been going strong since 1913 and has served their famous battered fried fish to a long list of celebrities from Mick Jagger to Tom Cruise and Edith Piaf. Crispy goodness in a paper bag! → p. 61

● *All about leprechauns*
Dive into Irish mythology in the *National Leprechaun Museum*. The museum's twelve interactive chapters take you through the history of the leprechaun – from the first sighting in the 8th century right through to today's representation in films and pop music → p. 103

● *In the world of film*
Three in one: the *Irish Film Institute* has a cinema – usually showing an interesting selection of movies – a very affordable café and a well-organised DVD shop → p. 73

RAIN

RELAX AND CHILL OUT
Take it easy and spoil yourself

● *Wellness with spring water*
The *Wells Spa* at the Hotel Brook Lodge only uses its own well water for their mud baths, massages and aromatherapy. If you are up to it, you can also take a very revitalising ice shower after one of your treatments → **p. 37**

● *A sanctuary of green*
Uncomplicated and free of charge, you can relax in *Phoenix Park* (photo), one of the largest inner-city parkland areas in the world. Covering an area of 1752 acres, there is more than enough space for a quiet picnic or an afternoon nap in the sun → **p. 50**

● *Massaged from head to toe*
Aches and pains do not stand a chance: three qualified therapists offer traditional Thai massages – oil massages, foot massages, shoulder and back massages as well as Indian head massages – at the *Mai Thai Massage* in the heart of the Temple Bar → **p. 37**

● *Getting the body into top form*
At *Therapie* your body will be whipped into fantastic form with a myriad of different treatments. Laser hair removal, specialist anti-wrinkle skin care treatments, beauty massages as well as laser eye treatments are all on offer. They even have a miraculous slimming tea → **p. 37**

● *Unwind to church music*
Even for non-believers a service in a Catholic cathedral can be very relaxing – especially on Sunday mornings when the magnificent *Palestrina Choir* sings the mass at St Mary's Pro-Cathedral → **p. 46**

● *Meditate on the masterpiece*
Michelangelo Caravaggio's painting 'The Taking of Christ' is the most significant exhibit at the *National Gallery of Ireland*. Avoid busy weekend opening times and spend a weekday relaxing on the padded seat in front of the painting and meditate on it for hours → **p. 32**

INTRODUCTION

DISCOVER DUBLIN!

James Joyce once described Ireland as 'the old sow that eats her farrow'. He found his hometown, the capital, too cramped and too Catholic, and he soon moved away, first to Paris, later to Zurich, where he is buried. With his epic novel, *'Ulysses'*, however, he created a *literary monument* that no other city has so far been able to claim. You can retrace the route that Leopold Bloom, its protagonist, walked on 16 June 1904; many of the places Joyce describes are still standing. By the way, the name of the city goes back to the Gaelic *Dubh-linn*: *'black pool'* and describes the basin area filled with dark water which formed where the rivers Liffey and Poddle (today an underground river) met and where the historic city settlement began.

The bleak period that drove many authors and artists abroad has long passed. Today the Irish capital, home to around one million people, is a *cosmopolitan, modern metropolis*, with much to offer locals, immigrants and visitors – including children. Where else would you find a museum inhabited by a leprechaun, a tiny shoemaker, who knows where a huge crock of gold is hidden?

Dublin is so compact that you don't need a car to explore the city. You can see almost everything comfortably by foot: *Trinity College* and its stunning library with the Book of Kells; the National Museum with its 'Celtic gold' collection; Georgian squares in the stylish south; the imposing walls of the Bank of Ireland and the castle; the main post office in O'Connell Street, Dublin's grand boulevard, where rebels proclaimed an Irish Republic in 1916; St Patrick's Cathedral, where Jonathan Swift, the *razor-sharp Irish satirist* who, quite tragically, most people only know for his novel, 'Gulliver's Travels', was once dean.

His regular haunt is still standing. The Brazen Head is *Dublin's oldest pub* (from 1614). The house is as crooked as can be and you have to stoop your head as you enter. The rebels of 1803 hatched their uprising in this pub, but, like so many before and since, it failed. The competition's *fervour to modernise* passed The

> ## Where the fiddle, accordion and *bodhrán* can be heard

Brazen Head by without a trace, the furnishings seem as old as the pub itself. There will usually be a couple of musicians, unknown artists, sitting in a corner playing traditional melodies on fiddles, accordions and bodhráns, an Irish drum. If you're lucky, there'll also be a bagpipe player to drown out the chatter of the patrons.

If you want to get to know the *'other Dublin'*, you simply must go to The Liberties. Here, in Dublin's oldest working-class quarter, you will find lots of antique dealers and small shops selling all kinds of odds and ends. The smell of Guinness, wafting

Live music sessions are the heartbeat of many pubs

over from the nearby brewery, hangs in the small streets of The Liberties, which has been home to many a *freedom fighter*.

Dublin is a *youthful city* with almost a third of its population under 25 years of age and the youth have given the city its vibrant rhythm and atmosphere and alongside the lovely old pubs are now chic modern bars and trendy clubs, especially in the *entertainment district* of Temple Bar, where the night glitters until morning breaks. The old quarter between Liffey and Dame Street, with its narrow, cobblestoned alleyways, was supposed to

Where the night glitters until morning breaks

make way for a bus station, but then lots of money was invested, the derelict houses were renovated and the *wasteland* was built on. Today it is bustling with boutiques, pubs and restaurants, Italian delicatessens and art galleries, clubs and rock cafés and the Film Institute with its bar, restaurant and art house cinema.

Dublin has become cosmopolitan. There are the immigrants with their *exotic shops* and restaurants, especially in the area around Parnell Street where there are a dozen (comparably cheap) Chinese restaurants. In Moore Street, a side street off Parnell Street, the old and the new Dublin sit side by side. This street, a pedestrian zone, is where fruit and vegetable traders – with the Irish gift of the gab – sell their produce from traditional wooden stalls as they have been doing for centuries. However, nowadays the rows of shops that line the street are in the hands of foreign folk: there are Nigerian and Chinese cafés, a hair salon with hair pieces for African women, a *Caribbean supermarket*. Even the butcher *FX Buckley's*, who has been running his business here for a hundred years, now sells *pig heads and tongues*, which are not something the Irish eat but which are prized by the Chinese.

Many immigrants stayed even after the economic crash, which lead to Ireland asking the European Union and the International Monetary Fund for help. In return, Ireland was forced to take drastic austerity measures. Five years later things started to pick up again. *Ireland's boom* was most evident in Dublin. The inner city's fallow areas were renewed with the construction of modern building complexes. The suburb of Smithfield, a working class district with narrow alleys and brick houses, was transformed. The place was

Once the grounds of a whiskey distillery, now a shopping paradise

given new cobblestone streets and modern street lamps, and on the massive site of an old whiskey distillery, a new world was born: *Smithfield Village* with luxury hotels, shopping arcade, Thai restaurant and 200 apartments. Or the Liffey: for hundreds of years the river was neglected and used as a rubbish tip, the buildings along its banks slid into decay and residents moved away. The urban revival saw the river transformed with a promenade, *wooden boardwalks* and a pedestrian bridge and now, on National Day on 17 March, there is also a fireworks display over the river. The largest development in Irish history got underway in the old harbour area, where apartments, hotels, parks, a conference complex and a shopping centre were created in the new district known as the Docklands.

The heart of the city is (and always has been) the area around the city's 400-year-old university, Trinity College, the chic shopping district around Grafton Street and the government district around Merrion Square and St Stephen's Green, whose *beautiful parks* are perfect for a lazy catnap, and there is way more space over in Phoenix Park, north-west of the centre, Europe's most extensive urban park. *Europe's tallest obelisk*, at 62 metres, stands next to the main entrance. Building began in 1817 in honour of the Duke of Wellington, who had defeated Napoleon just two years previously. However, the obelisk wasn't completed until over forty years later,

> **The area around Trinity College is the heart of the metropolis**

when Wellington was already long dead. The developers had run out of money by 1820 and apparently organised an *opulent dinner* for wealthy Wellington fans in the plinth of the obelisk in order to procure funding. After the meal, the vault was bricked up again. The story goes that many weeks had passed before the disappearance of a poor, drunken butler was noticed ... Dubliners like stories like like these, they make bland obelisks, for example, a bit more interesting.

If you are interested in stories in general and literature in particular, Dublin will seem like paradise. The city celebrates its writers in museums, theatres and on *Bloomsday*, the annual James Joyce Festival on 16 June, which has long since expanded into a week of festivities. Three authors from Dublin have won the Nobel Prize for Literature: William Butler Yeats, George Bernard Shaw and Samuel Beckett. A fourth, Seamus Heaney, made Dublin his adopted home. A monument was created to the authors in the shape of the Writers Museum. But the Irish love of storytelling is also writ large in the pubs. Here, at the latest, you'll find out that *pubs and culture* are not a contradiction. Experiencing pub culture is an essential part of any trip to Dublin.

Discussions in the pub are often about sports and politics, as well as specific politicians and stories from history. After all, Dubliners have also had a lot of experience with harsh economic and political upheavals, which run like a thread through the Irish capital's history. The *Vikings* founded the settlement on the Liffey in around 841, but were conquered by Irish King Brian Boru in 1014 and assimilated into the Celtic population. From 1170 Dublin was ruled by the British kings. From Dublin Castle, where you can now marvel at the State Apartments and the Chapel Royal, the British Crown set out to subjugate Ireland, which they finally managed to do after the Reformation. Thus began the era of *Protestant rule* over a predominantly Catholic country.

At the end of the 17th century, the narrow, impoverished alleyways of the Middle Ages gave way to broad streets and elegant squares lined with *prosperous Georgian townhouses* and buildings, like, for example, on Merrion Square, whose colourful house doors are typical of the era. A *period of peace and prosperity* for Dublin began. After the dissolution of the Irish parliament in 1801, Dublin lost its political and social significance. One rebellion after another was bloodily quashed by the English. The *Easter Rising* of 1916 failed after only five days – the rebels, who had holed up in the main post office on O'Connell Street, surrendered. But the mood turned after the brutal execution of the rebellion's leaders. The following two-year *War of*

Both cool and provocative: Dublin's storybook dandy Oscar Wilde resides in Merrion Square Park

Independence ended with the partition of the island. Dublin became the capital and seat of government with the formation of the Irish Free State in 1922. A crash course in Irish history is on offer at Kilmainham Gaol, where the rebels of the Easter Rising were executed. Volunteers began restoring the crumbling structure in 1960. Now it's a national memorial.

> **Where is there less rainfall – in Dublin or Nice?**

The weather certainly has stayed exactly the same, which is a good thing because the constant *rain* has served to protect the island from mass tourism and hotel tower blocks. There is a saying that the Irish have two favourite days of the year: Christmas and summer. This is an *exaggeration* as generations of holidaymakers have actually returned from Ireland with a suntan – it really is just a matter of luck – Dublin's annual rainfall is less than that of Nice's. The Irish also have another saying, 'A stranger is a friend you haven't met yet'. This is true of Dubliners, so go there and meet them!

1 Noodles or tapas?

Pasta basta Mother of all noodle bars is *Wagamama (South King Street)*. Here every conceivable kind of noodle is cut, twirled, slurped, be it rice or wheat, udon, soba or ramen. *Wagamama* paved the way for other cool noodle eateries like the *Wok Inn Noodle Bar (45–50 Stephen Street Lower)* which specialises in Thai. At *Yamamori Iza-kaya (12/13 South Great George's Street)*, the trend is to slap on a layer of East-meets-West in the form of Japanese tapas – Japas for short.

Bring your own

Goodbye wine list Increasing numbers of restaurants now operate without a liquor licence. And guests bring along their own wine. The *Dada (45 South William Street)* even forgoes a corkage fee with its Moroccan cuisine. Moustafa Keshk serves delicious home-style cooking at the *Keshk Café (71 Mespil Road)*. You select the wine for the oriental meal beforehand, for example at the *Boutique Wines (14/15 Trinity Street)*. Here you order the appropriate wine in advance so that your white is already chilled and the red decanted.

3 Emerald Isle

Eco Organic foods have conquered Dublin. You could try out the ✪ *SuperNatural Food Market (Sat 9.30am–3.30pm)* in Pearse Street or the *Farmers Market (Fri 11pm–3am)* in the Irish Financial Services Centre on the Liffey, where you'll find chocolate and olives alongside fruit and vegetables. At the ✪ *Edun (Brown Thomas & Co | 88–95 Grafton Street)*, U2 singer Bono and his wife Ali Hewson's fair trade fashion label, you can get items that are guaranteed to make you look good.

Dough with a hole

Iced delights Nowadays it's hard to imagine Dublin without the sweet, sticky ring of deep-fried dough known as the doughnut. It all began with the Dutch, who took their *olykoeks* (oil cakes) with them when they settled in New Amsterdam. The city is now called New York and is the hipster capital of the USA. In their most recent spell of popularity, quite possibly prompted by their biggest, yellow-faced fan Homer Simpson and now not quite so oily, the doughnut seems to have conquered the world. Dublin was apparently particularly prone to the craze. Around 20 shops, offering the most unbelievable varieties, opened within a year. In the past they were only available in supermarkets, and were considered boring and unhealthy. Nowadays they are still unhealthy, but are imaginatively decorated – and totally in. Check out *Offbeat Donuts (www.offbeatdonuts.com)* on George's Quay.

Pop-up spaces

Art on the go Empty factories and shops that are turned into a creative space. Eli McBett has taken over an old workshop and instead of an oil change there is now oil on canvas. The exhibitions at the *SHE-D (43 Gardiner Lane | www.mcbett.ie)* are constantly changing and are always worth seeing. To make spaces available to artists is also the aim of *Fillit (www.fillit.ie)*; this artists' initiative keeps investigating into exciting new projects, while the *Workmans Club (10 Wellington Quay)* has a proper (fixed) address where artists can work towards their breakthrough. It is also a venue for concerts, exhibitions and performances.

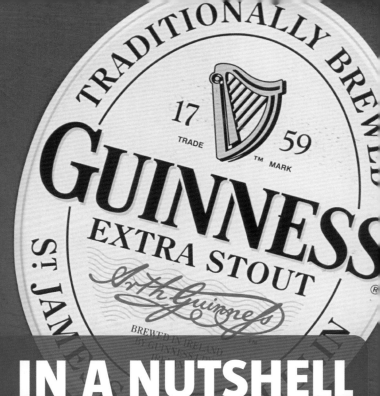

IN A NUTSHELL

A DAY OF THREE SEASONS

Trends come, trends go, but the weather is always a topic of conversation in Dublin. Don't let the rain get you down though, it's what safeguards the island from mass tourism – and that's the reason you came to Ireland in the first place, right? Anyone can lie on a sunny beach in Spain, but where else can you experience three seasons in one day? It rains often here, but rarely for very long. But that also means you can't really look forward to a fine day even if the sun is shining in the morning: 'Fine before seven, rain by eleven', as the saying goes. So be prepared for anything. A single remark about the weather will soon get you into conversation with a Dubliner.

FOR THE CRAIC

In Ireland, the pub is the focus of life. It is much more than just a place where you go to drink beer, rather it is a place that nurtures two very important elements of Irish culture: music and conversation. The importance of traditional music to the Irish is well documented, but even more important than the music is the conversation, as the Irish are a garrulous and humorous folk. Their eloquence has not only earned them the

What's the *craic*? Here you find all you need to know about shamrocks, Irish black gold and King George's favourite doors

Nobel Prize for Literature but it is also something that comes in handy every evening at the bar counter. And where there is Irish talk there is Irish laughter and so you will often hear the word *craic*, which is roughly translated as 'fun'. 'What's the *craic*?' can mean, 'What's going on?' or 'What's up?' and as a question it can also be a challenge to tell an entertaining and humorous story. After a successful evening at the pub you say, 'It was great *craic*!' – 'We had a lot of fun!'

LET'S GO TO LÁR

Tourists in Dublin often wonder how many buses drive to *An Lár* as it is not recorded on the city map. *An Lár* is the Irish word for the city centre. In Ireland Irish is, according to the 1937 Constitution, the country's first language, English only the second official language. However, the reality stands in stark contrast to this constitutional wish. Around 70,000 people in Ireland speak Irish regularly, and you'll find most of them in the 'Gaeltachts', regions where Irish is the primary language, and Dublin is one of them. The language is, however, threatened by extinction. That's a real shame – the experts assert that Irish Gaelic can express things with greater nuance and imagination than, for example, English. Take a listen to an Irish-language radio programme or the TV channel TG4 to get an impression of the sound of the language, even if you don't understand a single word. If you're feeling a little pressed and the toilet doors are labeled in Irish, you may be forgiven for assuming that 'Mná' means men, and 'Fir' therefore women, and consequently walking through the wrong door.

By now it's clear for all to see: you don't speak any Irish at all. You were told that doesn't matter, because the Irish speak the clearest colloquial English? Wrong. One of Dublin's winners of the Nobel Prize for Literature, George Bernard Shaw, did claim that the best English in the world is spoken in Dublin, but he probably only frequented the upper-class areas of the city. He's hardly likely to have heard, for example, the expression 'I need to hit the jax' there. It means: 'Please excuse me, I need to pay a visit to the bathroom'. But don't worry, Dubliners are patient and are happy to repeat themselves as often as is needed for you to understand them.

THE LONGEST DAY IN WORLD LITERATURE …

… begins around eight o'clock on the morning of 16 June 1904, when the 38-year-old advertising agent Leopold Bloom closes the door of 7 Eccles Street behind him and begins an eighteen-mile

IRISH ROUGHNECKS

The Irish are a sports-mad, competitive nation, something that is very evident during a live match of either one of their traditional Irish sports of *hurling* (with women: *camogie*) or *Gaelic football*. The most important games of the *All Ireland Football Championship* take place between April and September and those of the *National Hurling League* between February and April at
INSIDER TIP ▶ *Croke Park Stadium (Jones Road | northern suburb Drumcondra | tel. 01 8 36 32 22 | www.crokepark.ie)*, held by the *Gaelic Athletic Association*. The highlight of the season is the all-Irish finals on the first and third Sunday in September, also in Croke Park. Game fixtures are listed on the Gaelic Athletic Association's website *(www.gaa.ie)*. Besides football, the Irish also love rugby. A highlight for rugby fans is the *Six Nations Championship (Jan–March)* between England, France, Ireland, Italy, Scotland and Wales. The old *Lansdowne Road Stadium*, which was built in 1832 in the southern suburb of Ballsbridge, had to give way to the super modern 50,000 seater *Aviva Stadium (DART Lansdowne Road | tel. 016 68 46 01 | www.avivastadium.ie)*. Football is now also played there and it is where the Irish national football team play their home matches.

The city reclaims its master in the end: James Joyce in St Stephen Green

odyssey through Dublin, and ends when he returns at two the next morning. You too can try this feat, like many Joyce enthusiasts do every year, on Bloomsday, 16 June. Many of the stops on Bloom's path, which James Joyce described in his epic 'Ulysses', have survived, e.g. the Sandycove defence tower or Sweny's chemist's shop, where Bloom buys a bar of lemon soap. 'Chemists rarely move', Bloom correctly prophesies. The same goes for the dead in the Glasnevin Cemetery, where the novel's hero arrives in a carriage with three other mourners. The house on Eccles Street is no longer standing, but the door is now on display in the Joyce Centre. Joyce pilgrims tick off spots on the route like the Stations on a way of the Cross. The artist John Ryan decided to do it in style on the 50th anniversary of Bloomsday, renting a carriage to follow in Bloom's footsteps in the company of a couple of friends – including the writers Flann O'Brien and Patrick Kavanagh, and Tom Joyce, a cousin of the author. They only managed about half of the route before they were so drunk that they fell out. You'd be better off going for a Gorgonzola sandwich and a glass of

Burgundy at Davy Byrne's like Bloom does – now only available on Bloomsday.

TWELVE STRINGS FOR THE FILÍ

The twelve-stringed harp, Ireland's national emblem, stands for the Filí, the court poets of Celtic society, and therefore for Irish music and literature. When the flag – with a yellow harp on a blue background – is raised in Phoenix Park, it indicates that the head of state is at home (the state residence is right in the middle of the park). The harp is also seen as part of the stone coat of arms on the façades of some of the more prestigious buildings but it is most often seen as the Guinness logo. However, the Guinness harp is inverted because in Ireland it would be presumptuous to depict a state harp on a glass of beer.

IRISH BLACK GOLD

The pub is the Irishman's extended living room – all you need to do in a Dublin pub is raise your finger and you'll be served a Guinness without further ado. If you want to drink something else, you'll have to let them know explicitly. This despite the fact that the brewery's headquarters has long since been in London. Guinness is actually brewed in more than 150 countries and 40 percent of production is consumed in Africa. But it still tastes best in Dublin, because it doesn't have far to go – whether in a pub, a beer garden, at a traditional music session or in the Guinness Storehouse. The brewery grounds stretch along both sides of Thomas Street in The Liberties. With more than a just a hint of optimism, Arthur Guinness leased the brewery for 9000 years, for an annual rent of 45 pounds, on 31 December 1759. The original building was a mere four acres, today it covers over 64 acres, on which four million pints – each a magic 0.56 litres – are brewed every day. There is no way around it, you have to try one. If it's too bitter for you, give it another chance. And then another. After the fifth pint you'll have got used to it and won't want to drink anything else ever again.

EVERYONE'S CALLED GEORGE

Georgian architecture in Dublin dates from the period between 1714 and 1830, where four consecutive British kings were called George. At the time Dublin was the second most important city (after London) in the emerging British trade empire and the city experienced a period of prosperity and growth. The population grew from 60,000 to 224,000, and affluent new suburbs developed. They had wide streets, elegant squares and prestigious residences and homes in a characteristically classical style. The most striking aspect of the Georgian architecture is its famous Dublin doorways. The doors themselves are all painted in bright, bold colours and there are rarely two adjacent homes with the same colour door. The best example today is still Merrion Square.

STAY CALM – AND DRINK TEA

The Irish are world champions – at tea drinking. They drink it all the time, no matter the circumstance – many wouldn't even be functional without their seven or eight cups a day. Builders drink even more. According to a study, 70 percent of them find tea has a stress relieving effect. As a result, their productivity is increased. Builders in other countries are more likely to ascribe these attributes to beer. It has been calculated that the average amount of tea consumed during the construction of an Irish semi-detached four-bedroom house is 9500 cups. And it's the first thing you'll be offered when visiting a Dubliner. Take a packet home with you as a souvenir. Even the quality of the tea bags is excellent.

EXOTIC CITY

Dublin has become colourful. The cityscape is no longer characterised by the uniform rows of grey shops and the pale Irish, but rather by immigrants and their exotic shops – especially in the northern part of the city centre. Poles, Balts, Nigerians and 100,000 Chinese arrived during the economic boom at the end of the 1990s. Since then, Dublin has had its own Chinatown, though it's fairly modest compared to New York or London, being made up of a single street. The shops and restaurants lined up one after the other on Parnell Street are mainly used by Dublin's Chinese community. The dishes they serve take some getting used to for a European palate. But don't worry: they do sweet and sour chicken here too.

UISCE BEATHA – WATER OF LIFE

Whiskey is finally being distilled in Dublin again. The new distillery is called Teeling and you can view it in the old working-class district of The Liberties. It's about time – the traditional distillery Jameson moved away from the capital a long time ago. However, it left behind the old Jameson Distillery on Smithfield Market, where you can find out all there is to know about *Uisce Beatha* (Gaelic for 'water of life'). Because the soldiers of the British King Henry II, who occupied Ireland in the 12th century, could not pronounce the word, they corrupted it to whiskey. Irish whiskey (with 'e') has been available for more than a thousand years. The Irish are proud that they invented it, even though the Scots like to take credit for it. As proof, the Scots point out that there are far more Scottish brands than Irish, to which the latter reply that the Scots are 'still practising'.

THREE-LEAFED HALLELUJAH

The market gardens have their work cut out on St Patrick's Day, 17 March, the national holiday when every Dubliner wears the patriotic green of the shamrock in their lapel. Legend has it that Patrick picked up the three-leafed clover in order to explain the Trinity to the Irish during his missionary work in the fifth century. Now the three-leafed shamrock appears everywhere when the country's colours are flown, whether that be on the jerseys of the Irish national football and rugby teams, on the tail fin of Aer Lingus' airplanes or in the tourist board's logo.

When the Irish Prime Minister visits Washington on St Patrick's Day, as is now tradition, they always take a crystal bowl full of shamrocks as a gift for the US president with them. Meanwhile the Irish back home endeavour to 'drown the shamrock' in whiskey, as tradition demands. The patron saint of the Emerald Isle is venerated in every city and every village with music, street parties or fireworks – and of course parades. The biggest takes place in Dublin.

Not without my shamrock – this lady is ready for St Patrick's Day

SIGHTSEEING

WHERE TO START?
O'Connell Bridge (117 D3)
(∅ G4): This is a good vantage point from which to get a good overview of the city. North is O'Connell Street, the main thoroughfare, to the east is the old Customs House and the harbour, and to the west is the cast-iron Halfpenny Bridge. From here turn right into Fleet Street and you are in the heart of the city's cultural and entertainment district, Temple Bar. *Bus Burgh Quay/O'Connell Bridge | Luas Abbey Street*

If you have ever walked your legs off in London or Paris then you will really appreciate Dublin, as all the sightseeing attractions are very close to each other in the city centre. The highlights that are not near the city centre can be explored by taking a bus round trip. Dublin offers the tourist so much and yet everything is in a compact and manageable area.

The city's attractions cover all the aspects of its long history. Trinity College with its old library and the magnificent 1200-year-old Book of Kells, two medieval cathedrals (a European rarity) and elegant 18th-century squares and buildings, all chronicle the city's development from early

A city with heart and soul: forget about London, Paris or Rome – Dublin really does offer everything you need

Christian to modern times. It is also full of memorials dedicated to its many literary giants like James Joyce, Oscar Wilde and other famous poets. Meanwhile, the Dubliner's enjoyment of a good tipple is evidenced by the Guinness Brewery and Jameson Whiskey distillery and its many pubs. And their fight for independence is shown in places like Dublin Castle and Kilmainham Gaol.

A small country with a strong cultural history: the Emerald Isle can look back over 9000 years of cultural history and this is a treasure trove for the capital's museums. The city's excellent collections not only include the wealth of the past, but also showcase modern Ireland. Special insights into Irish passions are revealed at the sports museum at Croke Park Stadium, an introduction to Irish litera-

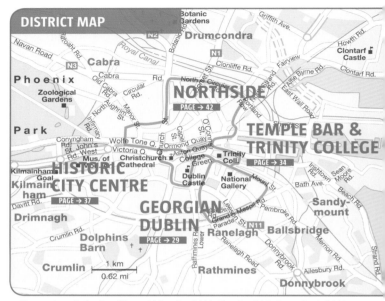

DISTRICT MAP

The map shows the location of the most interesting districts. There is a detailed map of each district on which each of the sights described is numbered.

ture is best obtained at Dublin Writers Museum while information about the city's history is at the City Hall and the Dublinia. But if you visit only one museum in Dublin, then your choice should be the National Museum of Ireland's Archaeology section, filled with the gold treasures that they discovered on the Irish moors and in burial sites. Another world-class institution is the Chester Beatty Library with its remarkable collection of precious manuscripts.

The city's most important sightseeing attractions can be reached with three bus stops all along the same route. Take a round trip with the INSIDER TIP Dublin Bus (www.dublinsightseeing.ie | 24 hour ticket 19 euros, online discount 15 %) and enjoy the live commentary and witty banter of their Dublin bus drivers. They

are humorous, irreverent and very well informed. Another option is the bright green buses from the Dublin Bus Tours (24 hour ticket 19, online 16.15 euros | www.dublinsightseeing.ie) fleet with a choice of either live commentary from the bus driver or headphone commentary. All operators offer discounts if you book online. But there are also plenty of tours through Dublin on foot or by boat (see p. 113).

If you buy a 24-hour bus round trip ticket, you can hop off and on directly in front of the following museums (in the order of the trip): National Gallery, Natural History Museum, National Museum – Archaeology, Chester Beatty Library, City Hall, Dublinia, Museum of Modern Art, National Museum – Decorative Arts, Dublin Writers Museum and The Hugh

Lane Gallery. There can be no easier route to enjoy a city's art, culture and history!

GEORGIAN DUBLIN

The Irish government has made its home in the splendid area around the elegant Merrion Square and St Stephen's Green. It was in this area in the 18th century that the Georgian architectural era flourished. The resultant streets have long, wide boulevards that are flanked by elegant townhouses for the prosperous. The area remains the city's most significant architectural treasure and it is no wonder that parliament, a number of ministries and cultural institutions like the National Museum are based here. The gorgeous gardens on the squares and the banks of the beautiful *Grand Canal* provide lovely relaxation areas.

1 GRAND CANAL

(122–123 A–F 1–3) (*E–J 5–6*)

The canal, completed in 1811, was originally an important connection between the city of Dublin and the river Shannon. Today, however, it is not industry that characterises the Grand Canal south of the city centre, but the picturesque bridges and locks, trees and elegant townhouses. The part between the Portobello district at Richmond Street and Mount Street Lower makes for an exceptionally beautiful walk along the water. This egg-shaped area, the Grand Canal in the South and its counterpart in the north, the Royal Canal, are boundaries of Dublin and only those born here can call themselves real

MARCO POLO HIGHLIGHTS

★ **Merrion Square**
Beautiful examples of Georgian architecture → p. 31

★ **National Gallery of Ireland**
Masterpieces from the late Middle Ages to the 19th century → p. 32

★ **National Museum – Archaeology**
Prehistoric gold treasures and precious objects from Ireland's Christian past → p. 32

★ **Trinity College**
Where learning blossoms: historic courtyards, the Book of Kells and a remarkable library → p. 36

★ **Chester Beatty Library**
Not just for book lovers: exquisite books from different cultures and epochs → p. 37

★ **Dublin Castle**
Where British viceroys resided in all their glory → p. 40

★ **St Patrick's Cathedral**
1500 years of history in its Gothic architecture and interior → p. 41

★ **Guinness Storehouse**
All about the famous stout beer – and some striking city views → p. 49

★ **Kilmainham Gaol**
A moving insight into Irish prison history → p. 50

★ **Phoenix Park**
A massive public park, the zoo and the head of state's residence → p. 50

Dubliners. *grandcanaldublin.com | DART Grand Canal Dock, Luas Charlemont.*

Afloat on the Grand Canal Basin is the INSIDER TIP *Waterways Ireland Visitor Centre* (123 E2) (*Ø H5*) *(April–Sept Mon–Fri 11am–4pm | admission 8 euros |*

Blood is thicker than water? Not on the Grand Canal

www.waterwaysirelandvisitorcentre.org | DART Grand Canal Dock). Discover the history of the Irish waterways, e.g. the race to the Shannon between the builders of the Grand Canal and the Royal Canal. Learn how to steer a barge and navigate through the locks.

2 INSIDER TIP IVEAGH GARDENS
(122 C3) (*Ø G6*)

In the middle of Dublin's inner city is an oasis of tranquillity that is often overlooked. Iveagh Gardens might be missing the flowers of the neighbouring St Stephen's Green, but there are many trees, two beautiful fountains carried by angels and spacious lawns perfect for Frisbee players. *Entrances at Clommel Street and Hatch Street Upper | Luas Harcourt*

3 LEINSTER HOUSE
(117 E5) (*Ø G5*)

It wouldn't be a surprise if you found the building somehow familiar. The first two stories as well as the facade of Leinster House served as the model for the White House in Washington, which was also designed by the Irishman James Hoban. The power emanating from within the two buildings, in Dublin and Washington, differs greatly, but the Irish Prime Minister actually earns more than the US president. The *Dáil* (lower house) and the *Seanad* (upper house) sit within the walls of the building built in 1745. The 30-minute tour is free, but it is best to book in advance as only the first 30 visitors are granted admission. *Mon–Fri 10.30am, and 2.30pm, when not in session (bring your passport with you) | 2 Kildare Street | tel. 01 6 18 32 71 or 01 6 18 37 81 | event. desk@oireachtas.ie | bus Nassau Street/ St Stephen's Green*

4 INSIDER TIP LITTLE MUSEUM OF DUBLIN (117 D6) (*Ø G5*)

The best little museum in the city – as the Irish Times described it – presents the history of the Irish capital in the 20th century over three floors. 'U2 – Made in Dublin' for example traces the success story of the band – including memorabilia such as a packet of U2 condoms. Looking at over 5000 exhibits, which were all (!) donated by the general public, can work up an appetite. There's ten percent off at Hatch & Sons if you show your museum ticket. *Daily 9.30am–5pm (Thu till 8pm) | admission 10 euros, guided tour*

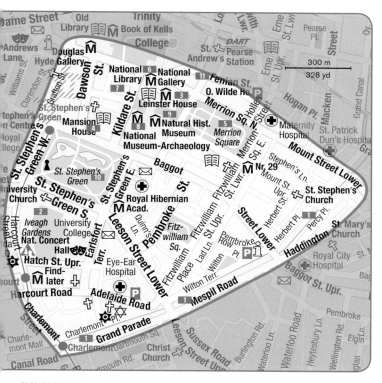

SIGHTSEEING IN GEORGIAN DUBLIN

1 Grand Canal
2 Iveagh Gardens
3 Leinster House
4 Little Museum of Dublin
5 Merrion Square
6 National Gallery of Ireland
7 National Library
8 National Museum – Archaeology

▨▨ Pedestrian precinct
9 Natural History Museum
10 St Stephen's Green
11 Sweny's Pharmacy

only (every hour, on the hour) | 15 St Stephen's Green | Luas St Stephen's Green

5 MERRION SQUARE ★ ●
(117 F5–6) (*⊞ G–H5*)

Since the 1770s, Merrion Square has been one of the finest addresses in Dublin. It is well known for its typically Georgian architecture, its colourful doors and the beautiful park in the middle of the square. There is also a collection of historical street

lamps and an old air raid bunker in the south-east corner. Daniel O'Connell (no. 58), William Butler Yeats (no. 84) and Oscar Wilde's family (no. 2 at the north-east corner, now the *American College* and infrequently open to the public) all lived in Merrion Square. For many years Wilde's books were banned in Ireland but now there is an unusual statue of him across from his former home. Oscar Wilde himself would have loved the colourful statue,

31

because it really does capture his persona very well. The dandy and man of letters is sprawled with provocative ease on a boulder, looking towards his family home. Among the houses built between 1791 and 1825 to line the adjacent, privately owned *Fitzwilliam Square* are some particularly fine examples of Georgian architecture. *Bus Merrion Square*

6 NATIONAL GALLERY OF IRELAND ★ (117 E5) (*① G5*)

It's not the Louvre, but the Irish National Gallery contains a top-class collection of art with masterpieces from all over Europe. The centrepiece is Michelangelo Caravaggio's ● 'The Taking of Christ'. You had better sit down on the bench in front of the painting to read this: at the end of the 18th century, the painting was considered lost and it remained that way for 200 years. Then it reappeared in 1990 in a Dublin Jesuit monastery. It had been hanging in the refectory there for 60 years, but was thought to be a vile copy. An Irish paediatrician had given it to the monks in thanks for their support after her husband, a policeman, was shot by the IRA. The National Gallery's conservator ultimately identified the painting as a real Caravaggio. The odyssey is over, it has finally found its place. Oh yes, there are also works by Tizian, Velazquez, de Goya, Picasso, Rubens, Nolde and other masterly painters in the National Gallery. But maybe you need a rest in the *museum café* after the Caravaggio. *Mon–Sat 9.15am–5.30pm (Thu until 8.30pm), Sun 11am–5.30pm | free admission | Merrion Square West/Clare Street | www.national gallery.ie | bus Merrion Square*

7 INSIDER TIP NATIONAL LIBRARY (117 E5) (*① G5*)

The old National Library next to the parliament building, Leinster House, isn't high up on most tourists' 'must see' list. You don't need to make the same mistake. Even if you aren't interested in books, the library is a feast for the eyes with its ornate lobby, the stairway to the large reading room, glass roof, cherub mouldings in vibrant colours and stucco ceiling. And if you don't want to leave, just pick up a book. The snazzy shelves with wood carvings and tables with green reading lamps belong to the original furnishings. *Mon–Wed 9.30am–7.45pm, Thu, Fri 9.30am–4.45pm, Sat 9.30am–12.45 pm | free admission | Kildare Street | bus Nassau Street/St Stephen's Green*

8 NATIONAL MUSEUM – ARCHAEOLOGY ★ ● (117 E5) (*① G5*)

If you wanted to fill an ark with all the objects that document Ireland's rich history, then you would use all the exhibits in this museum. Here you can see well-preserved Bronze Age weapons and horns (used as instruments) and some really remarkable gold treasures: wonderfully crafted collars, bangles, gold earrings and gold filaments. One of the rarities from early Christian times is the 1200 year-old *Ardagh Chalice* and the *Tara Brooch*, crafted around the year 700 and decorated with Celtic patterns. An ancient bog body, a dugout canoe dating from about 2500 BC, Viking finds and medieval artefacts are just some of its many highlights. The museum also houses a good Egyptology collection. *Tue–Sat 10am–5pm, Sun 2pm–5pm | free admission | Kildare Street | www.museum.ie | bus Merrion Square, St Stephen's Green*

9 NATURAL HISTORY MUSEUM (117 E5) (*① G5*)

Irreverent Dubliners call the museum the 'Dead Zoo'. At the entrance you are

The National Library: when architects pull out all the stops for umpteen books ...

greeted by the skeletons of some of the Irish elks that lived on the island 10,000 years ago. The *Irish Room* on the ground floor is dedicated to indigenous animals, while the top floor has stuffed specimens of animals from all around the world. Even after extensive renovations the museum has preserved its Victorian charm – it has remained a kind of museum within a museum. *Tue–Sat 10am–5pm, Sun 2pm–5pm | free admission | Merrion Street | www.museum.ie | bus Merrion Square West*

▨ ST STEPHEN'S GREEN
(117 D6) (*ጠ G5–6*)

The park is a gift to the people of Dublin from the Guinness brewery – presumably out of thanks for their diligent consumption of the dark beer. A lot remains of the original 18th-century buildings on the eastern side of the square. The other sides show, in varying degrees, post-1960s planning errors, but are still worth seeing, particularly for those interested in history: the imposing *Royal College of Surgeons* on the west side shows traces of the battles in 1916.

James Joyce studied in the Catholic University *Newman House (June–Aug Tue–Fri 2pm–5pm, tours 2pm, 3pm, 4pm | 5 euros)* on the south side, before he fled from the Catholic narrowness of his hometown. By the way, in the southeast corner is a memorial to 'Operation Shamrock', during which around 500 German children where sent to Ireland between 1946 and 1947, which was unveiled in the 1990s by the then President of Germany Roman Herzog. *Bus, Luas Street Stephen's Green*

▨ SWENY'S PHARMACY
(117 F5) (*ጠ G5*)

You may not need any lemon soap, but you should pay Sweny's a visit anyway.

Leopold Bloom bought that famous bar of soap for his wife Molly on 16 June 1904 in this shop, which originally opened as a pharmacy in 1853. Okay, neither Bloom nor Molly are real people, they are in fact creations of the Dublin author James Joyce, whose 'Ulysses' describes the longest day in world literature (see p. 22). But fiction beats reality: if you turn up at Sweny's on 16 June, you'll come across Joyce maniacs from all around the world, there, like you, to buy lemon soap.

By the way, one year after Sweny's opened, and only one hundred metres away at 21 Westland Row, Oscar Wilde was born. Sweny's is now a bookshop, which also sells works by, you guessed it, Joyce. You too can take part in the regular readings *(donation requested)*. And maybe someone will manage to explain 'Ulysses' to you. *Mon, Tue, Fri, Sat 11am–6.30pm, Wed 11am–5pm, Thu 11am–9pm | 1 Lincoln Place | sweny.ie | bus Davenport Hotel, Merrion Street*

TEMPLE BAR & TRINITY COLLEGE

Temple Bar **is both a cultural and an entertainment district. Immerse yourself in the individual flair and laid-back atmosphere of its cafés and shops during the day; in the evening, Temple Bar is the place for fans of film and music, but some areas are also notorious for partying.**

In the 1980s, the small alleyways and houses of the old merchant district were supposed to make way for a new bus terminal. But instead, the rundown and dilapidated area became a magnet for the creative set, the potential of the area on the Liffey was acknowledged, and a renovation that preserved the Temple Bar's character was begun. Right next to the buzzing Temple Bar are two venerable

Get in the flow: drift between party and pub in Temple Bar

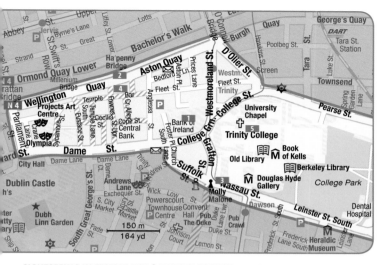

SIGHTSEEING IN TEMPLE BAR & TRINITY COLLEGE

1 Bank of Ireland
2 Halfpenny Bridge
3 Molly Malone Statue
4 Temple Bar Square
5 Trinity College

▨ Pedestrian precinct

institutions: the *Bank of Ireland* in the old Parliament building and the old university *Trinity College*.

■ BANK OF IRELAND
(117 D4) (ฌ G5)

The Capitol in Washington is only a replica. The original is here in Dublin. Everyone is welcome to stroll in to admire the wonderful main hall. Prepare to be astonished, as the building has gone through an amazing transformation: in the 18th century it was used as the Irish Parliament. At the time, windows were taxed – so they just left them out here. Tour guides with a lot of knowledge about Irish history lead tours through the House of Lords with crystal chandeliers, tapestries and Irish oak panelled walls. *Main hall Mon–Fri 10am–4pm, free tour only Tue 10.30am, 11.30am, 1.45pm | 2 College Green | bus College Green*

■ HALFPENNY BRIDGE
(116 C3) (ฌ G5)

You can cross this bridge free of charge. That wasn't always the case. The bridge was built in 1816 as Wellington Bridge but the toll (which was in place until 1919) gave it its present-day name of Halfpenny Bridge. The beautiful cast-iron 'Ha'penny Bridge', as Dubliners call it, connects the pubs and clubs north of the Liffey with the stone *Merchants Arch*, which leads into the Temple Bar district. *Bus Aston Quay, Bachelors Walk*

■ MOLLY MALONE STATUE
(117 D4) (ฌ G5)

During the day she sold fish, and at night she sold herself. According to legend, Molly was a fishmonger's daughter from Fishamble Street in Temple Bar, who died in 1699. But there is no proof that she actually lived. However, every Irishman

35

Half a year for 680 pages? The clocks tick more slowly in Trinity College Library

knows the ballad about the buxom beauty: 'In Dublin's fair city, where girls are so pretty, I first set my eyes on sweet Molly Malone ...'. *On the west side of Grafton Street near the entrance to Trinity College | bus Nassau Street*

▲ TEMPLE BAR SQUARE
(116 C4) (*M G5*)

This small, square is the heart of the Temple Bar district, surrounded as it is with small inviting pubs and restaurants. In the evening there is live music in many of the establishments while up-and-coming talents try their luck busking on the pavements. All hell breaks loose here at the weekend, when locals and tourists party until the sun rises. During the day and in the week Temple Bar Square and the adjacent alleys are civilized enough: the *Irish Film Institute* with its art-house cinema is only two minutes away in Eu-

stace Street. To the west on East Essex Street is the *Project Arts Centre*, with two stages and a gallery, while *Button Factory*, with studios and concert venue, is around the corner in Curved Street. On weekends a small book market is held on the square. More info: *www.visit-templebar.com | bus Aston Quay, Dame Street*

▲ TRINITY COLLEGE ★
(117 D4) (*M G5*)

It won't cost you anything to enter the university, founded in 1592 under the patronage of Elizabeth I, and those who study here don't pay fees either. It was the monarch's intention that her Protestant countrymen should not, at any cost, be 'infected with papism' and thus become 'degenerate subjects'. Thus, for more than two hundred years, the university only educated Protestant students – as decreed by the state. Famous alumni are writers such as Jonathan Swift, Dracula creator Bram Stoker, Oscar Wilde and Samuel Beckett. By the way, the library also contains a book that will take you almost half a year to read, no matter how fast you are. The Book of Kells is a 680-page exquisitely illustrated handwritten manuscript of the four Gospels. It is believed to have originated around the year 800 on the Scottish island of Iona and was then given to the monastery of Kells (in county Meath) to safeguard it against Viking raids. One page is turned every day. After 170 days the time finally comes to close the cover.

A flight of stairs leads up to the spectacular, barrel vaulted *Long Room*, where about 200,000 manuscripts are kept. Particularly impressive are the wood carvings on the high bookshelves, the line of busts of Irish writers and scientists and the oldest Irish harp, which dates back to the late Middle Ages. *May–Sept Mon–Sat 8.30am–5pm, Sun 9.30am–5pm, Oct–April Mon–Sat 9.30am–5pm, Sun mid-day–4.30pm | admission Book of Kells and Long Room: 10–13 euros | College Street | www.tcd.ie | bus Nassau Street, College Street*

HISTORIC CITY CENTRE

In the Middle Ages the trading city of Dublin extended a mile south from the river Liffey and the city's ancient main roads still exist today as Dame Street, Lord Edward Street and High Street.
To the left and right is evidence of the city's chequered past, like its two medieval cathedrals and Dublin Castle, where the British tried to rule Ireland for 750 years. But times have changed. Today the area is partly a shopping and tourist district, but also has commercial office buildings, apartments and homes.

■ CHESTER BEATTY LIBRARY ★
(116 B5) (𝄞 F5)
For many, the visit to this library is actually the highlight of their Dublin trip. This museum was a gift to the Irish nation from the American mining millionaire Sir Alfred Chester Beatty (1875–1968) and houses unique objects, manuscripts and exhibits from a number of different cultures. Among the highlights are papyrus

TIME TO CHILL

Those in need of relaxation can opt for the luxurious wellness spa at the edge of the Wicklow Mountains, an hour's drive south of Dublin: ● *Wells Spa* (0) (𝄞 0) (*Macreddin Village | tel. 0402 3 64 44 | www.brooklodge.com*) at the *Brook Lodge* Hotel. Finnish baths, aromatherapy baths and hammam massages ensure total relaxation. The pool water is from the hotel's own wells. In the city you can be pampered with the massage and beauty services at ● *Therapie* (117 D5) (𝄞 G5) (*9 Molesworth Street | tel. 01 4 72 12 22 | www.therapie.ie*) or at the *Merrion Hotel* (117 E6) (𝄞 G5) (*Upper Merrion Street | tel. 01 6 03 06 00 | www.merrion hotelcom*). At Temple Bar you can relax at ● *Mai Thai Massage* (116 C4) (𝄞 F5) (*41 Wellington Quay | tel. 01 532 84 20 | www.maithaimassage.ie*) with their traditional Thai practices.

scrolls from the year 200 with the gospels of Mark and Luke, precious Koran exhibits from Turkey, Iran and India, wonderful Buddhist and Far Eastern book art. And it also includes rare jade writings from the Chinese imperial court, medieval manuscripts and early European print specimens. The museum regularly presents different temporary exhibitions with treasures from its archives. A good idea for a break would be the INSIDER TIP *Silk Road Café* in the atrium of the Chester Beatty Library, offering exclusively homemade dishes and cakes. What's more, you can buy food from the Middle East and the Mediterranean region there, too. *Tue–Fri 10am–5pm, Sat 11am–5pm, Sun 1pm–5pm, May–Oct also Mon 10am–5pm | free admission | on the grounds of Dublin Castle | entrance at Dame Street or Ship Street | www.cbl.ie | bus Dame Street*

2 CHRIST CHURCH CATHEDRAL
(116 B4) (*ω F5*)

Although Ireland is predominantly Catholic, there are two Protestant cathedrals in Dublin, only a stone's throw from one another. This is because the city limits once ran between Christ Church Cathedral and St Patrick's Cathedral. Christ Church Cathedral, which is more than 800 years old, underwent extensive restoration in the 19th century and was remodelled in the early Gothic style. The cathedral has INSIDER TIP two curiosities: the first is a display case with the mummified remains of a cat and a rat, which were found in an organ pipe. The second is in the south-east Peace Chapel where there is a heart-shaped relic made out of iron, which houses Archbishop Laurence O'Toole's heart. He died in 1180 and was sanctified in 1230. *Mon–Sat March and Oct 9am–6pm, April–Sept 9.30am–7pm,*

Dublin's City Hall ... a wonderful place to tie the knot!

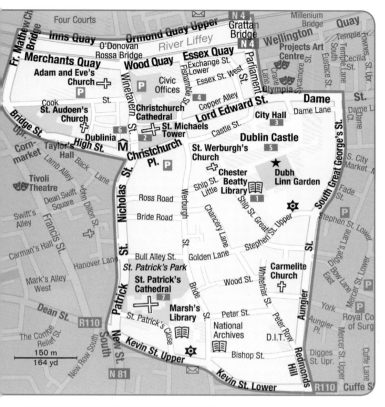

SIGHTSEEING IN THE HISTORIC CITY CENTRE

1 Chester Beatty Library
2 Christ Church Cathedral
3 City Hall
4 The Contemporary Music Centre
5 Dublin Castle
6 Dublinia
7 St Patrick's Cathedral

Nov–Feb 9.30am–5pm, Sun March–Oct 12.30pm–2.30pm and 4.30pm–6pm, Nov–Feb 12.30pm–2.30pm | admission 6.50 euros | Christchurch Place | www.christchurchcathedral.ie | bus Lord Edward Street

3 CITY HALL (116 B4) *(ꞯ F5)*

If you happened to decide to get married during your trip to Ireland, this would be a wonderful place to do it. Just rent the City Hall for the ceremony, it isn't that expensive. Dublin's merchants had the classical dome building erected as a stock exchange in 1779 but in 1851 it became the City Hall. The rotunda has an impressive dome and is also where you can see a 6 m/19 ft high statue of Daniel O'Connell, the city's first Catholic mayor (since the Reformation) in 1841. If you do end up getting cold feet, just divert the wedding party to the vaulted cellar, where audio-visual presentations convey a detailed picture of Dublin, e. g. in the times of the Vikings and Normans, during the Middle Ages and in its heyday in the 18th century. Truth be told, it's not quite as exciting as saying 'I do'. *Mon–Sat 10am–5.15pm | Dame Street/cnr Parliament Street | admission 4 euros | www.dublin city.ie | bus Dame Street*

■4 THE CONTEMPORARY MUSIC CENTRE (116 B4) (*ﬄ F5*)

If you want to fully immerse yourself in contemporary Irish music, then head on over to the Contemporary Music Centre. With its huge archive and well-furnished library, there isn't a question on the subject that can't be answered there. The Centre supports composers and artists. You can even buy their scores here, if you just can't get by without music from the island. By the way, the Music Hall where Georg Friedrich Handel premiered his Messiah once stood in Fishamble Street. *Mon–Fri 10am–5.30pm | admission free | 19 Fishamble Street | www.cmc.ie | bus Dame Street*

■5 DUBLIN CASTLE ★ (116 B4) (*ﬄ F5*)

The year was 1684. A huge blast shook the whole city. The gunpowder storage room in Dublin Castle had exploded. Only a 13th-century round tower survived, otherwise there is nothing left to see of the drama, as a wonderful Georgian palace grew out of the rubble. A further drama didn't come to such a happy end: in 1907 the Irish Crown Jewels were stolen from the castle and have never resurfaced. Dublin Castle was a building fit for the representatives of the British monarchy, including its own jail: the rebels of 1798, among others, were imprisoned in Bermingham Tower until their deportation to Australia. After the War of Independence and the foundation of the Irish Free State in 1922, the British representatives were forced to leave the country, but their portraits remained and still adorn the walls. The Irish government now uses the castle for representational purposes, for the inauguration of presidents or for meetings of the European Council. You simply must see the glittering ballroom and the banquet hall with all its gilded furniture. *Daily 9.45am–5.45pm, Sun midday–4.45pm | admission 7, guided tour 10 euros | Dame Street | www.dublin castle.ie | bus Dame Street*

LOW BUDGET

These outstanding Dublin facilities all offer free admission: the *National Museum – Archaeology,* the *National Museum – Decorative Arts and History*, the *National Gallery of Ireland*, the *Natural History Museum*, the *Chester Beatty Library*, the *Irish Museum of Modern Art* and the *Hugh Lane Gallery (Tue–Thu 9.45am–6pm, Fri 9.45am–5pm, Sat 10am–5pm, Sun 11am–5pm | Parnell Square North | www.hughlane.ie | bus Parnell Square).*

The *Dublin Bus* 'Leap Card' (about. leapcard.ie/about/fares-discounts) can be charged in many shops. Use it to travel by bus, DART and Luas for cheaper, without having to carry the right change; the 3 day *DoDublin Card (33 euros)* also includes a round trip with commentary. Both available at the airport and 59 Upper O'Connell Street.

6 DUBLINIA (116 A4) (*☐ F5*)

It was a crime against culture of international proportions. When workmen began digging up an area along the Liffey to build new office blocks for Dublin city make do with a copy. Dublinia is made up of recreated scenes and audiovisual displays. But the visit is still worth it, especially for the vivid representation of the Vikings' lives with their ships, tools and

Explosion, robbery and British viceroys ... Dublin Castle has been through a lot

council in 1974, they came across structures from the original Viking settlement: streets, houses, workshops with tools, some of which were made of organic matter. It was possibly the most important Viking find ever uncovered. Archaeologists from all around the globe feverishly rummaged through the soil for artefacts, trying to save what was in fact already lost – despite mass demonstrations, supreme court judgements and heartfelt appeals from scientists from all over the world, the office blocks were built, burying the most important testimony to Dublin's early history beneath them. So unfortunately you're going to have to weapons. *Daily March–Sept 10am–6.30pm, Oct–Feb 10am–5.30pm, admission 9.50 euros |St Michaels Hill, Christ Church Cathedral | www.dublinia.ie | bus Lord Edward Street*

7 ST PATRICK'S CATHEDRAL ★
(116 B6) (*☐ F5*)

Not many people find their final resting place in a four-story grave. The Boyle family certainly must have been important to have been buried in such a cenotaph. The grave of the razor-sharp satirist and dean of the church, Jonathan Swift, creator of Gulliver, is plainer. His 'Stella' lies nearby, in the middle of the nave.

The Anglican St Patrick's Cathedral was built in the early 13th century in the Gothic style in place of the older buildings, which possibly go back to the wooden church of St Patrick. The wooden door in the north transept has an unusual history attached to it: during a feud between the Earls of Ormond and Kildare in 1492, Ormond locked himself in the cathedral's chapter house. Kildare wanted to end the conflict so he knocked a hole into the door and put his hand through as a peace offering.

St Patrick's Park next to the cathedral is the place – according to tradition – where Patrick converted and baptised 450 people to Christianity and it is a pleasant place for a break. Niches in the wall on the east side of the park are dedicated to important Irish writers. *March–Oct Mon–Fri 9.30am–5pm, Sat 9am–6pm, Sun 9am–10.30am, 12.30pm–2.30pm, 4.30pm–6pm, Nov–Feb Mon–Fri 9.30am–5pm, Sat 9am–5pm, Sun 9am–10.30am, 12.30pm–2.30pm | admission 6.50 euros | St Patrick's Close | www.stpatrickscathe dral.ie | bus Patrick Street*

NORTHSIDE

The area north of the Liffey riverbank combines various historical aspects of the Irish capital, so this is where you will find medieval Dublin (St Michan's Church), Georgian Dublin (the Custom House) as well as 18th-century stately homes.

The chic hotels and bars in the immediate vicinity of the river are reminders of Dublin's financial boom years, whilst a few streets away the buildings are still waiting to be restored to their former glory and the department stores with their cheap prices. This district offers you a vibrant and colourful mix of interesting museums, the wide boulevard of *O'Connell Street* and some good theatres.

Nowadays you don't have to be converted to stop off in St Patrick's Park

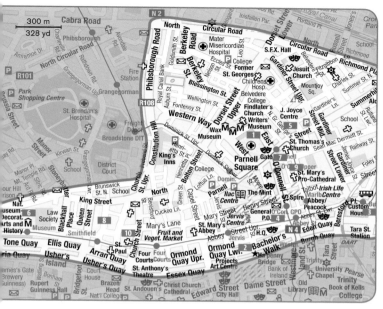

SIGHTSEEING IN NORTHSIDE

1. Dublin Writers Museum
2. Dublin's Last Supper
3. EPIC – The Irish Emigration Museum
4. General Post Office
5. James Joyce Centre
6. National Museum – Decorative Arts and History

Pedestrian precinct

7. O'Connell Street
8. Old Jameson Distillery
9. St Mary's Pro-Cathedral
10. St Michan's Church

1 DUBLIN WRITERS MUSEUM
(120 C5) (*∭ F4*)

Which city of Dublin's size can boast three winners of the Nobel Prize for Literature? Alongside William Butler Yeats, George Bernard Shaw and Samuel Beckett, a fourth prizewinner, in the shape of the Northern Irishman Seamus Heaney, also lived in Dublin. The Writers Museum is dedicated to Ireland's literati, many of whom had been banned and cast out in the past, e.g. Oscar Wilde and James Joyce, who surely deserved the Nobel Prize too. The history of Irish literature is displayed with curiosities including a letter from George Bernard Shaw in which he refuses to give an autograph, but then signs the letter himself. The *Irish Writers Centre* next door at no. 19 holds readings and seminars. *Mon–Sat 9.45am–4.45pm, Sun 11am–4.30pm | admission 7.50 euros, combined ticket 11.50 euros for the Dublin Writers Museum and the James Joyce Museum | 18 Parnell Square | www.writersmuseum.com | bus Parnell Square*

2 INSIDER TIP DUBLIN'S LAST SUPPER
(116 C3) (*∭ F5*)

Dublin's Last Supper, the Irish version of Leonardo da Vinci's masterpiece, represents the changes within Irish society and

Seagull at Millennium Spire – best keep your eyes open …

its new cultural diversity. The large artwork from 2004 is in a courtyard in Dublin's *Italian Quarter*, somewhat hidden on the Liffey, and was created by the Northern Irish artist John Byrne. It consists of 13 photographs of locals, whom Byrne met on the streets of Dublin. *Blooms Lane | Lower Ormond Quay | Luas Jervis*

3 INSIDER TIP EPIC – THE IRISH EMIGRATION MUSEUM
(117 F3) (*QU G4*)

Did you know that Barack and Michelle Obama (O'Bama), Che Guevara and Muhammad Ali all have Irish roots? Once you've taken a look at the interactive exhibition, across 20 different galleries, on the history of Irish emigration and the influence of emigrants from the Emerald Isle around the world, you'll no longer be surprised. And who knows, maybe you'll discover an Irish ancestor too. The brother of the great-grandfather of your grand-aunt on your mother's side …? *Daily 10am–6.45pm (last admission 5pm) | admission 14 euros | Custom House Quay | epicccq.com | DART Connolly*

4 GENERAL POST OFFICE (GPO)
(117 D2) (*QU G4*)

The main post office was used as the headquarters of the rebels during the 1916 Easter Rising and has since become a national shrine. After its destruction in 1916, the neoclassical building was restored by the Irish government. Its counters, post boxes and tables – made from marble, dark wood and shiny brass – make it worth a visit. On the façade outside you can still see bullet holes. In case you need stamps, and there is a long queue at the post office, it is worth going into the INSIDER TIP *Philatelic Office* to the right of the main entrance. It is usually empty and you can get beautiful commemorative stamps here. *Open during business hours | O'Connell Street | bus O'Connell Street*

5 JAMES JOYCE CENTRE
(120 C5) (*QU G4*)

You haven't read 'Finnegan's Wake' and put down 'Ulysses' after the first page? Then join the club. Nonetheless, you may still be interested in the life and work of the Dublin eccentric, who emigrated while still young but always remained connected to his hometown through his writing. The James Joyce Centre offers temporary exhibitions as well as lectures, seminars and guided walks. *Mon–Sat 10am–5pm, Sun midday–5pm (Oct–March Mon closed) | admission 5 euros | 35 North Great George's Street | www.jamesjoyce.ie | bus O'Connell Street*

6 NATIONAL MUSEUM – DECORATIVE ARTS AND HISTORY
(122 A1) *(🗺 E4)*

The splendidly restored 18th and 19th century *Collins Barracks* served as barracks for almost 300 years. Today they house a significant art collection, which covers all the areas of the applied arts: weapons, furniture, ceramics, fashion, silver and glass from many different centuries. Temporary exhibitions highlight different themes from Irish history. The INSIDER TIP *Curator's Room* is a great source of inspiration for any visitor. Here the museum's curators show and explain their favourite pieces. *Tue–Sat 10am–5pm, Sun 2pm–5pm | free admission | Benburb Street | www.museum.ie | bus Patrick Street | Luas Museum*

7 O'CONNELL STREET
(117 D1–3) *(🗺 G4)*

Dublin's impressive thoroughfare honours the gifted politician who fought for the equal rights of Catholics in the first half of the 19th century – Daniel O'Connell (1775–1847). His memory is celebrated by an impressive memorial on the south side of the street. The street was left to decay for decades and was dominated by the neon signs of hamburger chains and other cheap establishments. After extensive renovations the street is once more deserving of its reputation as a grand and imposing boulevard. One of the most remarkable monuments is on the median strip, the *Monument of Light* (also called the *Millennium Spire*), a 120 m/392 ft high, impressive shining steel needle that sparkles over Dublin's rooftops at night. Detractors say it's a monument to Dublin's heroin addicts. Admiral Nelson looked down on this spot from a pillar until 1966, but on the 50th anniversary of the 1916 Easter rising, the IRA blew up this symbol of British rule.

8 OLD JAMESON DISTILLERY
(122 B1) *(🗺 F4)*

Distilling whiskey is more complex than you might think. The visitor centre, in the disused distillery, offers some good insights into the fine art of whiskey distilling. The tour, which includes sampling, doesn't hold back on promoting the product, but is nonetheless entertaining and informative. *Smithfield Square*, where you could once buy reasonably priced fruit

FIT IN THE CITY

With an area of 1750 acres, Phoenix Park is double the size of New York's Central Park, giving you plenty of space to run! The ambitious can go full circle (11 km/7 mi) but there are shorter routes throughout the park or you can also take a bicycle ride: *Phoenix Park Bike Hire (Chesterfield Ave | tel. 08 62 65 62 58)*. If you would rather smell the sea air, drive to the coast where Malahide Beach **(125 F4)** *(🗺 0)* has great running tracks. Swimmers who dare to enter the chilly waters of the Irish Sea best do so at *Forty Foot* **(125 F5)** *(🗺 0)* in Sandycove. In the middle of the city centre you'll find the *Markievicz Leisure Centre's* the swimming pool **(117 E3)** *(🗺 G5) (Mon–Thu 7am–9.45pm, Fri 7am–8.45pm, Sat 9am–5.45pm, Sun 10am–3.45pm | admission 7 euro | Townsend Street near Trinity College | DART Tara Street).*

A whiff of the big wide world beyond blows over the Samuel Beckett Bridge in Docklands

and vegetables in the market halls, has now been completely renovated, and new apartments have been cleverly integrated into the old buildings around the distillery. A relic of times gone by is the *horse market*, which takes place twice a year (March and Sept). Occasionally, the square is the venue for concerts in all manner of musical styles. *Distillery Sun–Thur 10am–5.30pm, Fri–Sat 10am–7pm | admission 20 euros | Smithfield Village | Luas Smithfield*

9 ST MARY'S PRO-CATHEDRAL
(117 D2) (*M G4*)

Church incognito: The 'provisional' Roman Catholic cathedral is hidden away down a side street. Only after the emancipation of the Catholics in 1829 were their churches allowed to be part of the cityscape. St Mary's was built in 1816 in the Greek style with modest proportions.

During Sunday mass, the multi-award-winning ● INSIDER**TIP** *Palestrina Choir* performs here *(11am). 83 Marlborough Street | bus O'Connell Street*

10 INSIDER**TIP** ST MICHAN'S CHURCH
(116 A3) (*M F4*)

Prepare yourself for a blood-curdling encounter at this 17th-century church. The main attraction are the underground vaults. The tannin-rich air of the church's crypts have mummified the corpses buried there and prevented their decay. One of the corpses in the macabre display apparently belongs to a crusader who you used to be allowed to shake by the hand, as it was supposed to bring good luck. This has now been banned, in the crusader's interest. The main rooms of the church upstairs aren't quite as unsettling, but instead opt for a bit of named-ropping: Wellington, who later defeated

docks, ports and storage warehouses at the Liffey near the city centre became too small for modern merchant ships, the old harbour district slowly declined. In the course of the economic boom at the start of the 1990s, however, the old buildings were transformed into modern palaces of steel and glass. The Docklands is now considered a landmark development that serves as a reminder of Ireland's economic boom time when it was one of Europe's wealthiest countries. Some of the main attractions in this area are architect Daniel Libeskind's *Grand Canal Theatre* (which is now named *Bord Gáis Energy Theatre* after its sponsor), the *Convention Centre* with its glass atrium, the *Samuel Beckett Bridge* as well as *Point Village.* It is also where you will find *3 Arena (North Wall Quay | tel. 01 8 19 88 88 | Luas The Point)*, a Victorian warehouse, which has been specially converted for concerts into a kind of amphitheatre for 14,000 visitors, offering superb acoustics. The programme can be found under *www.3arena.ie.* On the north side of the Liffey, east of the Custom House, are the *Famine Statues*, a modern memorial to the lives lost in the terrible famine in the mid-19th century. One million Irish died because the British government continued to export cereals and meat from Ireland to Great Britain, irrespective of the potato blight that had devastated crops. Another million fled the famine to the USA. The tall ship *Jeanie Johnston*, a reproduction of one of these 'famine ships', is anchored at the Sean O'Casey Bridge. *DART Connolly Station | Luas Connolly Station*

Napoleon, was baptised in the font and Georg Friedrich Handel used the organ keyboard in the foyer for the world premiere of his Messiah in Dublin. *Tours March–Oct Mon–Fri 10am–12.45pm and 2pm–4.45pm, Nov–March 12.30pm–3.30pm, Sat all year round 10.30am–4pm | admission 5 euros | bus Church Street | Luas Four Courts*

IN OTHER DISTRICTS

DOCKLANDS
(117 F2) (*ØØ G–J4*)
The Mutiny on the Bounty and Dublin's harbour have more in common than you might think: parts of the harbour were actually designed by William Bligh, the captain of the Bounty. But when the

THE LIBERTIES ●
(122 A–B2) (*ØØ E–F5*)
The Liberties is the oldest working-class district in the Irish capital and is steeped in the historical flair of an anarchistic sub-

urb: the area once lay outside the city walls and was not subject to municipal law. It thus had, until 1840, the freedom to run its own courts as well as to levy customs and taxes. They also allowed themselves other freedoms: rebels planned uprisings and founded socialist parties in the small, red-brick houses and alleyways. Today, the Liberties, with its pubs, small shops and street traders, is one of the liveliest areas Dublin has to offer. By the way, the smell of Guinness pervades the air here. The big, blue gates have lined both sides of Thomas Street since the brewery expanded at the end of the 18th century. The antithesis of the chic shopping area – around Grafton Street in the centre – is *Liberty Market (Thu–Sat | 71 Meath Street)*, where you can find inexpensive groceries and clothing alongside household items and communion dresses. *St Augustine Church* on Thomas Street is a marvel of neo-Gothic architecture built in 1862–95. The interior is opulent and colourful: stained glass windows, a white Carrara marble altar, colourfully painted holy statues and mosaics turn the church into a sparkling treasure. *Bus 13, 40, 123 Thomas Street*

MORE SIGHTS

GAA MUSEUM
(121 D4) (*∅ G3*)

Sport and politics don't mix? They do in Ireland! The GAA (Gaelic Athletic Association), which preserves and promotes traditional sports, was part of the resistance against the British occupation since its foundation at the end of the 19th century. That's why the interactive GAA Museum inside Croke Park Stadium isn't only about sport. Watch a game of Gaelic football – a sport only remotely related to football as you know it – or hurling, which is only remotely similar to hockey. The rules for both can be explained quite quickly: the aim is to score goals. A goal gets you three points. If the ball goes over the bar and between the extended posts, you get one point. This rule means that

A game of hurling in Croke Park, and all of Dublin is here

the game can become an infinitely boring affair for the goalkeeper, but not for the spectators. Both sports are fast-paced; hurling is actually considered the fastest game on grass. *Jan–May and Sept–Dec Mon–Sat 9.30am–5pm, Sun 10.30am–5pm, June–Aug Mon–Sat 9.30am–6pm, Sun 10.30am–5pm | admission (museum only) 7 euros, stadium tour incl. museum 14, family ticket 38 euros | St Joseph's Avenue | Croke Park | www.crokepark.ie/ gaa-museum | bus 123, 130 from O'Connell Street*

GLASNEVIN CEMETERY
(120 A2–B2) (*[map] E2*)
The mission statement of this cemetery, which hangs at the entrance, is to 'Preserve the Past for Future Generations'. The cemetery – officially known as *Prospect Cemetery* – is Dublin's answer to the Père Lachaise in Paris. More than 1.2 million people are buried here: the rich and the powerful, the famous and the infamous, the poor and the unknown. The founder of the cemetery, Daniel O'Connell, is buried in a crypt under the replica of a round tower near the main entrance. Many gravestones in the old part of the cemetery carry Celtic crosses with the sun symbol, others are unintentionally funny: a married couple holding an inverted wine glass, with their feet resting on an empty wine bottle, are depicted on the gravestone of an abstainer. The cemetery is as secure as a fort with a 4 m/13 ft high wall with watchtowers which were used as protection against grave robbers. Fresh corpses were worth a lot of money at the beginning of the 19th century when physicians needed a constant supply for their anatomical examinations. After the round trip, a break in the cosy *Kavanagh's* pub at Prospect Square is recommended. It is commonly known as the *Gravediggers* pub. *Daily 9am–4.30pm, guided tours 11.30am and 2.30pm | 8 euros | Finglas Road | bus 40, 40B, 40D, 140 from Parnell Street.* The INSIDER TIP *Glasnevin Museum (daily 10am–5pm, Sat–Sun 11am–5pm | admission 6.50 euros, combined ticket cemetery tour and museum 13 euros | www. glasnevinmuseum.ie)* below the souvenir shop is worth a visit: it was awarded a prize as best international museum.

GUINNESS STOREHOUSE ★
(122 A2) (*[map] E5*)
Find out how Guinness is made in the converted 19th-century factory building. As well as learning about the brewing process, you will also hear all kinds of anecdotes about Irish black gold. For example: An expedition to the North Pole in 1927 apparently found four bottles of Guinness that another research team had left behind 18 years previously – the brew was of course still drinkable. And the visit to the Storehouse doesn't stay dry either: in the *Gravity Bar,* a glass rotunda on the roof, you can enjoy a free pint of Guinness and the best view of the city. *Daily 9am–6pm | admission 14–20 euros, depending on the time of day, advance online booking recommended | St James' Gate | www.guinness-store house.com | bus 13, 40, 123 from D'Olier Street | bus 40 from O'Connell Street*

IRISH MUSEUM OF MODERN ART
(119 E6) (*[map] D5*)
In the past, the imposing old Royal Hospital Kilmainham up on the hill, with views of the river and a beautiful, 18th-century-style garden, was a retirement home for British war veterans. Now the estate is dedicated to culture and houses the national collection of modern art. The museum has been collecting artworks since 1990 and has some top quality temporary exhibitions. *Tue–Fri 11.30am–5.30pm, Sat 10am–5.30pm, Sun 12am–*

5.30pm | free admission | www.imma.ie | 5 min on foot from Heuston Station; to get there take the Luas red line and buses 13, 40 from D'Olier Street

KILMAINHAM GAOL ★ ●
(119 D–E6) (*∅ D5*)

When Kilmainham Gaol opened in 1796, it was praised for the improved conditions for its prisoners – unimaginable when you look at the bare, drafty cells now. A guided tour through the prison is a crash course in recent Irish history. If there are English tourists taking part, the guides really go to town and are particularly vociferous in reproaching the British atrocities in Ireland. The prison was full of Irish rebels, from the day it opened, a good 200 years ago, until it closed in 1924. One of them was Éamon de Valera, the only leader of the Easter Uprising who wasn't executed, because he held an American passport. He was the last prisoner in Kilmainham, later he became the head of government and president of the Republic of Ireland. After his release, the building was abandoned. In 1960 a group of volunteers began its restoration. The adjacent exhibition gives you a good overview of the Irish struggle for independence from 1798–1922. *Daily June–Sept 9.30am–6.45pm, Oct–May 9.30am–5.30pm | admission 9 euros online (online booking recommended) | Inchicore Road | www.heritageireland.ie | bus 69 from Aston Quay*

NATIONAL BOTANIC GARDENS ●
(120 B2) (*∅ F2*)

At the ripe old age of 200 years, the Botanic Gardens, in the sheltered valley of the River Tolka, may, by rights, have been dead and buried long ago. But a huge variety of exotic species from all over the world keeps it alive and kicking. Palms and orchids grow in the only remaining original Victorian greenhouses. In the meantime, the connecting door in the wall to Glasnevin Cemetery has been reopened, so that you can view both in comfort if you want to turn your back on Dublin's roaring traffic for a little longer. *Mid-Oct–Feb Mon–Fri 9am–4.30pm, Sat/Sun 10am–4.30pm, March–mid-Oct Mon–Fri 9am–5pm, Sat/Sun 10am–6pm | free admission | Botanic Road | www.botanicgardens.ie | bus 83, 83A from Westmoreland Street*

PHOENIX PARK ★ ● ☼
(118–119 A–E 1–5) (*∅ A–D 1–4*)

After a night of partying in Temple Bar, the fresh air of Phoenix Park is an ideal way to clear the mind. Europe's biggest city park was once the royal red deer reserve. There are still deer, but today Phoenix Park also accommodates sports meetings and other big events. 120,000 guests attended the Robbie Williams concert but Pope John Paul II attracted the largest crowd, an estimated 1.2 million, in 1979. At the entrance an obelisk honours Wellington's victory at Waterloo, north-west from there is the head of state's residence, right in the centre of the park. The *Dublin Zoo (daily March-Sept 9.30am–6pm, Oct–Feb reduced hours, core time 9.30am–4pm | admission 17.50 euros, children 13 euros)* is situated in the east of the park. *Park open all day every day | bus 25, 26, 66, 67 from Wellington Quay | Luas Museum or Heuston, then about 10 min on foot*

WHERE TO GO

DUN LAOGHAIRE/KILLINEY/ SANDYCOVE (125 F5) (*∅ 0*)

The ● DART, takes you from Connolly Station in as little as 30 minutes to other places of interest on the coast south

Simply turn your back on the urban hustle and bustle in Dublin's Botanic Gardens

of Dublin. The *James Joyce Museum (daily 10am–4pm | free admission, donation requested | www.jamesjoycetower. com)*, housed in the Martello Tower in *Sandycove* is a cultural highlight on this stretch of coast. If you haven't read his opus then take 'Ulysses' with you and read the first chapter on the turret roof, as this is where it plays out. If the book does not captivate you here on site then it never will! The highlight – literally – is the ↘ *Killiney Hill summit* with wonderful views over the coast and mountains. A number of restaurants in *Dun Laoghaire* or Sandycove sell refreshments, for the more daring the cold water of the Irish Sea awaits at the *Forty Foot* bathing area.

HOWTH
(125 F4) (*ω 0*)
Travel north with the DART from Connolly Station to the terminus Howth – you won't regret it. The beautiful town centre, good seafood restaurants and the fresh sea air of a boat trip are always worth a day out. Incidentally, instead of the DART

you can also take the slightly slower bus (line 31 B) from Abbey Street or Connolly Station – the ↘ INSIDER TIP bus trip with panoramic view from the top deck is much more scenic. Behind the former Deer Park Hotel, of which only the golf course is still in business, a footpath, lined with rhododendron bushes, gently rises up to ↘ ● *Howth Head*. From here you have a great view over Dublin Bay and the city.

MARLAY PARK
(125 E5) (*ω 0*)
The 120 ha Marlay Park has everything you need to relax: forested areas, footpaths, ponds. If you're in need of a little more action, swing a golf club, tennis racket or cricket bat, or play football, Gaelic or otherwise. Afterwards reinvigorate yourself in the cafe or finally get your gift shopping done in the art and crafts shop. *Daily Nov–Jan 9am–5pm, Oct, Feb–March 9am–6pm, April 9am–9pm, Mai–Aug 9am–10pm, Sept 9am–8pm | free admission | 16 Grange Road | Rathfarnham | bus Marlay Park*

FOOD & DRINK

It sounds like paradise. Irish waters supply oysters, prawns and fresh fish, while lush green meadows provide tender beef and lamb, and more and more farmers are now producing organic vegetables. Yes, this is Ireland.

It wasn't so long ago that the island was seen as something of a culinary backwoods. Fortunately that's over now. The ingredients are first class, in the meantime the chefs are too, so there's nothing stopping you from exploring Ireland's specialities. Why not try the hearty *Irish stew*, usually made with mutton or lamb. Or perhaps *bangers*, as they call sausages around here, with mashed potato. Mash is also the main ingredient of *colcannon*, along with cabbage, butter and

spring onions, and often served with a thick slice of cooked ham.

If you're still unsure and prefer to rely on dishes you know, Dublin has many high-quality international restaurants on offer. The pleasure comes with a price though. In a mid-range restaurant you should expect to pay 30 euros for a three-course meal – not including drinks. But you can make your money go further if you know a couple of tricks.

Many pubs, for example, offer affordable meals, and not only at lunchtime. The INSIDER TIP pre-theatre menu is an early bird special that makes fine dining accessible in the evenings: patrons arriving from 5pm can order at a discounted price, but have to leave by 7pm or 8pm. Whether

Between Irish stew and haute cuisine: Dublin's culinary diversity is as captivating as the city itself

you really go to the theatre afterwards is, of course, up to you.

You should try *fish and chips* at least once while you're in Dublin, and preferably from a 'chipper', a local take-away. The best take-away is *Leo Burdock* near Christ Church Cathedral. The long list of international celebrities who have already gotten their hands greasy here is impressive. Furthermore, this meal is a good foundation for the following visit to the pub.

Take note of these times before your stomach starts to rumble: Dublin's restaurants generally serve lunch between midday and 2pm, dinner from about 6.30pm until 10pm, sometimes until 11pm. Details of differing opening times are found with the addresses in this edition. Pubs mostly open as early as 11am and close at 11.30pm during the week and at 0.30am on Fridays and Saturdays. Many places in the city centre have a special licence to open until late.

CAFÉS

AVOCA (117 D4) (*m G5*)

The delicious baked goods from their own bakery are irresistible and lure in both passersby and the local office workers

INSIDER TIP **BLAS CAFÉ** (116 B2) (*m F4*)

The chef hails from Morocco; you can tell as much from the menu – for example, Eggs Berber, Merguez sausages, cardamom cake. At lunchtime there are two types of sandwich with meat and

Bewley's Café serves good coffee in elegant surroundings

from the surrounding streets, ensuring the café is always full. If you go there before or after lunchtime you will be able to enjoy a good cup of coffee and a bite to eat without a reservation. *Closed in the evenings | 11 Suffolk Street | tel. 01 6 72 60 19 | bus Dame Street*

BEWLEY'S CAFÉ (117 D5) (*m G5*)

Its Egyptian-looking façade conceals the chic, renovated café. Breakfast rolls, freshly baked in the in-house oven, and afternoon teas are served in an elgant atmosphere with crystal chandeliers and dark wood. In the *Oriental Room* there are theatre performances during the day, jazz and cabaret in the evenings. *78 Grafton Street | bus Nassau Street*

two vegetarian varieties, plus a different warm dish every day. The prices in the *Chocalate Factory* are reasonable by Dublin standards. The atmosphere is unconventional. A seat on the red plush sofa is a particularly suitable spot to relax after your sightseeing activities. 'Blas' is the Irish word for taste, and there's certainly no shortage of that in this café! *Closed Sun and in the evenings | 26 King's Inn Street | www.blascafe.ie | bus Parnell Square West*

THE CHURCH ★ (116 B3) (*m F4*)

Cappuccino and a toasted sandwich in a church? The converted 18th-century church with its wooden panelling, commemorative plaques, organ and glass painting offers some great ambience. In the evenings the former St Mary's Church turns into a trendy club with restaurant *(the steaks are a must | Moderate– Expensive)* on the gallery and a spacious terrace. *Daily | Mary Street | tel. 01828 0102 | www.thechurch.ie | Luas Jervis*

INSIDER TIP THE FUMBALLY ⊘
(122 D5) *(ⅲ G5)*

One of the best places in Dublin for breakfast and lunch, if you like local and organic food. How about a probiotic, fermented cabbage and ginger juice or a green smoothie – all homemade of course? The owners even make their own vinegar from the leftover fruit pulp. That's what I call sustainable! If just reading that makes you shiver in disgust, they've got craft beer and cider too. The falafel wrap (6 euros) and pulled porchetta (6.50 euros) are among the food favourites.

A themed dinner is available on Wednesdays (approx. 25 euros, book!). An experimental kitchen is located in the Stables next door, which was built to house the horses used by the local breweries and distilleries in 1750. This is where the drinks are brewed. Take a look inside. *Tue–Fri 8am–5pm, Sat 10am– 5pm (kitchen closes at 4pm), Wed dinner 7pm–9.30pm | Fumbally Lane | tel. 015298732 | www.thefumbally.ie | bus Clanbrassil Street*

GELATO DI NATURA ★
(117 D2) *(ⅲ G4)*

With so many cool varieties, this shop is sure to melt the heart of any ice-cream lover. Preferably outside in the sunshine with a cone full of sorbet or dulce de leche, dark chocolate or mysterious exotic flavours. *Daily | 6 O'Connell Street Upper | Luas Abbey Street | bus O'Connell Street*

RESTAURANTS: EXPENSIVE

BANG
(117 E6) *(ⅲ G5)*

The stylish and beautiful Dublin in-crowd love this fine-dining minimalist restaurant, which serves modern Irish cuisine: besides their refined version of bangers and mash there is also foie gras or gravlax and Irish seafood deliciously combined with ingredients from the Mediterranean or the Orient. *Mon–Fri from 5.30pm, Sat/Sun from 5pm | 11 Merrion Row | tel. 01400 4229 | www.bangrestaurant.com | bus Luas St Stephen's Green*

MARCO POLO HIGHLIGHTS

★ **The Church**
Café in a converted old church – in the evenings it turns into a trendy club → p. 54

★ **Heron & Grey**
No windows and very small – but fantastic, scintillating cooking → p. 56

★ **Gelato di Natura**
The scoops are so big, the varieties so delicious, you're going to have to come again → p. 55

★ **Restaurant 101 Talbot**
Irish-Mediterranean cuisine in a relaxed atmosphere → p. 58

★ **Chapter One**
Dublin's perfect showcase for contemporary Irish cuisine → p. 56

★ **Dunne and Crescenzi**
Enjoy some Italian fare in amongst the groceries → p. 60

CHAPTER ONE ★ (116 C1) (f F4)

Tasteful literature: 'modern Irish cooking' in the *Dublin Writers Museum*. Do you fancy lobster-filled ravioli, or would you rather have local *Aberdeen Angus* steak with mushroom gratin? No matter what you choose, you can't go wrong in one of the best restaurants in the city. A three-course meal in the early evening costs 39.50 euros. *Closed Sun, Mon | 18–19 Parnell Square | tel. 01 8 73 22 66 | www.chapteronerestaurant.com | bus Parnell Square*

HERON & GREY ★ (125 E5) (*Ⓜ*)

The room isn't exactly promising: no windows and only enough space to seat 24 guests. But if you manage to be one of them (book far in advance and let them know if you require vegetarian dishes), then your taste buds are in for a treat. The food is the best that Dublin currently has to offer. The Australian chef Damien Grey and his Irish business partner Andrew Heron change the menu almost daily, because they only use the best ingredients for their modern and international cuisine (menu over 60 euros). The journey to Blackrock is worth it, not only for the Michelin stars – work up an appetite before an opulent dinner with a long walk through the coastal village. *Evenings only (closed Sun/Mon) | 19a Main Street | Blackrock | tel. 01 2 12 36 76 | www.heronandgrey.com | DART Blackrock (20 min journey)*

KING SITRIC ⚖ (125 F4) (*Ⓜ O*)

The Viking King Sitric would certainly not have dined as finely as the guests at this seafood restaurant on Howth harbour where you can enjoy wonderful sea views from the first floor. The menu does include beef and chicken dishes, but it

The boat restaurant MV Cill Airne: a decommissioned ship that has not land on the scrap yard

would be a real shame not to order some fish or other seafood here, as everything at the King Sitric is freshly caught. Besides lobsters and oysters, they also serve turbot and Dublin Bay prawns. The Irish cheese platter is a highly recommended option to round off the meal. *Wed–Sat from 6.30pm, Sun 1pm–5pm | East Pier | Howth | tel. 01 8 32 52 35 | www.kingsitric.ie | DART Howth*

MV CILL AIRNE (123 E1) *(Ø H4)*

A decommissioned training ship is the location for the *Quay 16 Restaurant*, the *Boat Bar & Bistro* and the *White Bar*. The kitchen serves contemporary European dishes, with a distinct emphasis on meat and fish, with vegetarian meals being the exception. There is a 'smart casual' dress code, so leisurewear and trainers are an absolute no-go. For safety reasons children are not allowed to come on board. *Quay 16 | North Wall Quay | tel. 01 4 45 09 94 | www.mvcillairne.com | Luas Spencer Dock*

RESTAURANTS: MODERATE

INSIDER TIP BAR ITALIA (116 C3) *(Ø F5)*

This is a good choice for some delicious and authentic Italian cuisine – the minestrone is as remarkable as the gnocchi and you will be hard pressed to find a better espresso in Dublin. Once you're well nourished, nip over the bridge, straight to the nightlife of the Temple Bar district. *26 Lower Ormond Quay | tel. 01 8 74 10 00 | www.baritalia.ie | bus Ormond Quay | Luas Jervis Street*

HARBOURMASTER (117 F2) *(Ø G4)*

A pub and restaurant – in what was once the harbour master's office in the Docklands – that is a popular choice with bankers from the surrounding finance district. The atmospheric building, with its wooden benches and rough brick, houses

a pub that serves simple dishes while the chic extension building serves up international cuisine with Irish influences. *Customs House Dock | tel. 01 6 70 16 88 | Luas Connolly Station*

KOH (116 C3) *(Ø F5)*

Situated directly on the Millennium Walkway, the pedestrian street leading from the Liffey to the Luas station Jervis Street, the Koh is a Thai restaurant and cocktail bar. The restaurant specialises in modern Thai cuisine with some unusual combinations (e.g. peppercorn duck with green pepper, gai lan, limes and red chilli). The ultra-modern dining room offers separate areas for private dinners. When the

LOW BUDGET

Reasonably priced Asian restaurants can be found in Dublin's growing Chinatown on Parnell Street in the section east of Parnell Square and on Capel Street.

Why not go the self-catering route and go shopping in the supermarkets in the Jervis or *ILAC Centre* **(116 C2–3)** *(Ø F4)* or the small Spar shops and then enjoy a picnic in one of Dublin's parks?

Many pubs serve meals from soups to roast beef at midday until early evening. The portions are plentiful and the prices (by Dublin's standards) are really reasonable. An excellent option: *The Brian Boru* **(120 B3)** *(Ø F2)* *(9 Prospect Road | www.the brianboru.ie | bus 40, 40B, 40D, 140 Hart's Corner)* near the Glasnevin Cemetery.

restaurant closes, you can move over to the cocktail bar for an hour or two. *Daily |6–7 Jervis Street | Millennium Walkway | tel. 018 14 67 77 | www.koh.ie | Luas Jervis Street*

RESTAURANT 101 TALBOT ★
(117 D2) (*M G4*)

Classic Italian pasta dishes and Irish beef. Fresh fish from local waters is served in Mediterranean style, e.g. halibut in *salsa verde*. Due to its location – in the shopping area around O'Connell and near the Abbey and the Gate Theatre – 101 Talbot is usually already quite full by early evening (book in advance!). *Closed Sun, Mon, Pre-Theatre Menu from 5pm | 101 Talbot Street | tel. 018 74 50 11 | www. 101talbot.com | Luas Abbey Street*

THE WINDING STAIR 🕙
(116 C3) (*M F5*)

The Winding Stair started out as a bookshop, and you can still buy new and antique books here. Wonderful stories may be enough to nourish a bookworm, but gourmets are more likely to appreciate the contemporary and organic Irish fine-dining cuisine that is now being served here. Indulge in the delicious Irish

FAVOURITE EATERIES

Gourmet for the adventurous

Have you ever tried steamed salmon in chicken grease, duck heart or blackened aubergine? If you're after culinary adventures, then *The Greenhouse* **(117 D5)** (*M G5*) *(closed Sun/Mon | Joshua House | Dawson Street | tel. 01 6 76 70 15 | www.thegreenhouserestaurant.ie | Luas St Stephen's Green | Expensive)* is the place for you. The very brave choose the surprise menu (5 courses for 85 euros), which star chef Mickael Viljanen creates for his guests on Friday and Saturday. Those who prefer to know what awaits them should visit any other day and choose the four-course menu for 79 euros or the six-course menu for 95 euros. Cheaper at lunchtimes and midweek (book in advance!).

Burgers of Dublin

Burgers with green Thai curry mayonnaise, peanut-chilli sauce or red onion chutney: if you ever needed proof that burgers aren't boring, then 🕙 *Jo'Burger* **(116 C5)** (*M G5*) *(daily | 4/5 Castle Market | www.joburger.ie | Bus South Great George's Street | Budget)* – delivers, in the form of twenty different exciting varieties. The lean meat is organically produced from Charolais cattle and has been hung to dry-age for 28 days. If you don't like beef, there's lamb, fish, chicken or even veggie burgers too. Branches: *Smithfield (10 Duck Lane)*, *Rathmines (137 Rathmines Road)*

Vinyl ambience

The Vintage Kitchen **(117 E3)** (*M G4–5*) *(closed Sun | 7 Poolbeg Street | tel. 01 6 79 87 05 | www.thevintagekitchen.ie | Dart Tara Street | Moderate)* serves up all your favourite vinyl cuts. Bring your own or choose from the restaurant's sizeable collection. Oh, you're here for the food? It's modern Irish fare. For 1 euro you get as much still or sparkling mineral water as you can drink. You can even bring your own bottle of wine (3 euros corkage fee). Book in advance!

mussels or the charcuterie plate or Dingle Bay crab. Depending on your choice the starter and main meal cost about 35 euros. *Daily | 40 Lower Ormond Quay | tel. 01 8 72 73 20 | www.winding-stair.com | bus Ormond Quay | Luas Abbey Street*

YAMAMORI NOODLES ★
(116 C4) (*ⓜ F5*)

Here you'll be served Japanese noodle dishes, soups and sushi in a stylish interior. This is also a good option for vegetarians or those wanting to grab a bite before setting off on a pub crawl in the area north of Dame Street. *Daily | 71/72 South Great George's Street | tel. 01 4 75 50 01 | www.yamamorinoodles.ie | bus South Great George's Street*; another branch is *Yamamori Sushi* (108 C3) (*ⓜ F5*) *|(38–39 Lower Ormond Quay | tel. 01 8 72 00 03 | Luas Abbey Street)*

RESTAURANTS: BUDGET

BESHOFF'S ♨ (117 D2) (*ⓜ G4*)

Some people think that Leo Burdock's fish and chips are a bit better, but Beshoff's also is a real Dublin institution in terms of fritters. It has a great view from the first floor on to the busy hustle and bustle of O'Connell Street down below. The interior is surprising: classical pillars, colourful stained glass windows and comfortable seats all create a surprisingly upmarket ambience for a fish and chip shop. *Daily | 6 O'Connell Street Upper | www.beshoff restaurant.com | bus O'Connell Street | Luas Abbey Street*

INSIDER TIP LE BON CRUBEEN
(117 D–E2) (*ⓜ G4*)

The street may not be one of Dublin's most attractive boulevards, but the restaurant – within walking distance of the Abbey and the Gate Theatre –

is highly rated by the locals. Find out for yourself with pork-belly confit and homemade burgers in a casual atmosphere. The three-course menu costs only

Jo'Burger packs as much as is physically possible between two halves of a bun

24.95 euros in the early evening (5pm–6.30pm). *Daily from 5pm, Mon–Fri also lunch midday–4.30pm | 81–82 Talbot Street | tel. 01 7 04 01 26 | www.leboncru been.ie | bus O'Connell Street | Luas Abbey Street or Connolly Station*

BROTHER HUBBARD ⊙
(120 B6) (*ⓜ F4–5*)

This small, cosy café in Capel Street in which, unlike in certain US establishments, they brew up a decent coffee, also offers a short menu. But it really packs a punch. For breakfast there's a selection

LOCAL SPECIALITIES

Bangers and mash – typical pub meal of grilled sausages with mashed potatoes (photo left)

Boxty – pancakes made using a mixture of potatoes, flour and either buttermilk, egg or butter (photo right)

Coddle – a casserole of potatoes, onions, bacon and sausage

Colcannon – mashed potatoes with cabbage, milk, cream, leeks or onions

Dublin Bay Prawns – fished in the waters of Dublin Bay

Fish and chips – this may be the English national dish, but the Irish have put their patriotism aside and love their battered and fried fish fillet with salt and vinegar chips

Irish breakfast – the full version includes fruit juice, cornflakes or muesli, scrambled eggs, fried bacon and sausage, black and white pudding (blood and liver sausage), baked beans and tomatoes, finished off with plenty of toast with jam; you get strong tea or coffee with it. Eat one of these and you won't need lunch

Irish stew – casserole of lamb with potatoes, carrots and onions

Pie – pies, sweet or savoury, are an Irish staple. Especially delicious: fish pie. Or round a meal off with an apple pie.

Stout – dark top-fermented beer, like Guinness or Murphy's

Whiskey – the Irish kind often tastes smoother than the Scottish. The most famous brands are Jameson and Bushmills and their characteristic flavour and quality are still as good as ever. There are also many other small producers.

of baked items straight from the oven; for lunch, they serve tasty salads, sandwiches (e.g. with artichokes, peppers and fried-tomato paste) and soup; in the afternoon you can try their home-made cakes. And evenings there's the 'Middle East Feast' for two. The emphasis here is firmly on fresh produce, where possible from organic cultivation. *Closed Mon |*

153 Capel Street | tel. 014 411112 | www. brotherhubbard.ie | Luas Jervis

DUNNE AND CRESCENZI ★
(117 D5) *(ﾉﾉ G5)*

Italian flair, good quality food, reasonable prices and its position near Trinity College and Grafton Street all make for a recipe for success for this wine & grocery store and restaurant. The menu is not extensive, but there is a selection of antipasti, panini and small dishes that vary daily. Inside you are seated between shelves full of Italian wine and pasta, and you can enjoy some sun and a glass of Prosecco at the tables in the front. *Daily | 16 South Frederick Street | tel. 01 6 77 38 15 | www.dunneandcrescenzi.com | bus Nassau Street*

GALLAGHER'S BOXTY HOUSE
(116 C3) *(ᗡ G5)*

Favourite address for fans of the Emerald Isle's traditional cuisine, and its comfortable traditional Irish atmosphere makes it a great place for you to discover the tastes of colcannon, coddle and boxty pancakes. The pancakes have a variety of rich and hearty fillings. *Daily | 20 Temple Bar | tel. 01 6 77 27 62 | www.boxtyhouse. ie | bus Temple Bar*

LEO BURDOCK ● (116 B4) *(ᗡ F5)*

Fish and chips fans argue about which establishment is the best but when it comes to celebrity clients, this small shop near Christ Church Cathedral wins hands down. A large board next to the shop entrance lists some of its world-famous clients: Edith Piaf, Mick Jagger, Sinead O'Connor, Bruce Springsteen, Venus & Serena Williams, Naomi Campbell, Russell Crowe and many more. The generous portions can be bought as a take away and then enjoyed on a nearby bench in Dublin Castle gardens or in front of the cathedral. *(Branches at 4 Crown Alley/ Temple Bar and 3 Mahers Terrace/Dundrum) Daily from midday | 2 Werburgh Street | bus Lord Edward Street*

INSIDER TIP ▶ MARKET BAR
(116 C5) *(ᗡ F5)*

The entrance of Market Bar may not be particularly pretty. But don't make the

mistake of walking by, because behind the unassuming façade lies one of the most stylish bars in Dublin. A café by day, a tapas bar by night or simply a hip and

You can't leave Dublin without trying fish and chips and a pint

happening place to enjoy a glass of wine. What was once a market hall and sausage factory has been converted into an airy space with rustic benches under the high vaulted glass and iron ceiling. The lack of music – very unusual in Dublin! – means an evening of conversation and *craic*. There's a cocktail bar on the first floor. *Daily from midday | 14a Fade Street | tel. 01 6 13 90 94 | www.marketbar.ie | bus South Great George's Street*

SHOPPING

CITY WHERE TO START?
Grafton Street (117 D4–5)
(🗺 G5): The best parts of this elegant shopping street are in the pedestrian zone and in the adjacent streets to the west up to South Great George's Street and in the east up to Kildare Street. Ideal for high-quality fashion, art and jewellery, books and CDs, souvenirs and groceries. *Luas St Stephen's Green | bus 32, 41*

A shopping trip is always fun and in Dublin it is even more so because its main shopping area, south of the Liffey, is very compact with everything in easy walking distance.

If you have some extra money to burn, go and do some shopping on Grafton Street. You'll find everything here to please a refined taste, for example in the exclusive department store Brown Thomas. There are plenty of pubs and cafés here, too, for whenever you need a rest from shopping. Afterwards, onwards to the small designer shops of Temple Bar, just a couple of minutes walk away. Bargain hunters romp north of the Liffey. In the side streets off O'Connell Street, for example Henry Street and its extension, Mary Street, you will find what you're looking for without having to take out another loan. In Earl Street you will find a row of shops which all sell inexpensive clothing and cheap Asian imports. Only those on the lookout for some special

WINES ON THE GREEN

Fine Wine Store

So much for Celtic kitsch:
discover how stylish, tasteful and
beautifully creative the Irish can be

antiques will have to head out of the city centre and go towards Francis Street in the Liberties. Those who enjoy reading or collecting old books will find an antiquarian book stall every weekend at the *Temple Bar Food Market*.

As far as prices are concerned, they differ widely in Dublin, so you should avoid impulse buying and first shop around and compare prices. Souvenirs are available on every street corner in the centre and also in the INSIDER TIP museum shops. As most well-known Irish whiskeys cost more

in Ireland than they do elsewhere, whiskey-lovers are better off buying their favourite tipple at home – unless you're looking for something special.

ART & MUSIC

ALL CITY (116 C4) *(∅ F5)*

If vinyl's your thing, you simply must visit this shop. But if you're more interested in visual art than music, then go anyway: the shop has a gigantic selection of affordable artist equipment – in particular

Powerscourt Centre: from elegant Georgian townhouse to exclusive shopping centre

spray cans for street art. *Daily | 4 Crow Street | bus Dame Street*

CLADDAGH RECORDS (116 C4) (*ΩΩ F5*)
Founded over 50 years ago to promote traditional Irish music, Claddagh Records is still one of the leading shops for Celtic music. *2 Cecilia Street | bus Temple Bar*

JAM ART FACTORY (116 C4) (*ΩΩ G5*)
Original, funny pieces of art don't have to be expensive. You will find something for bank accounts of every size here: unusual design and art by Dublin artists, such as felted shells and necklaces made of clay and glass. But even if you don't buy anything, it's fun just browsing amongst all these crazy ideas. *Daily | 14 Crown Alley | bus Dame Street (branches: Patrick Street 6/65)*

INSIDERTIP MOJO RECORDS
(116 C3) (*ΩΩ G5*)
At the end of Halfpenny Bridge under the *Merchants Arch* is a true paradise for music lovers. In this tiny record store you will find exactly those records that have been on your wish list for years – whether CD or vinyl. There are also DVDs, music posters and memorabilia. Mojo Records specialises in Irish rock. *4 Merchants Arch | Temple Bar | bus Ormond Quay*

WALTON'S WORLD OF MUSIC
(116 C5) (*ΩΩ F5*)
In this charmingly old-fashioned shop you can kit yourself out with traditional Irish musical scores and buy yourself an Irish drum *(bodhran)* or a small tin whistle. *69 South Great George's Street | bus South Great George's Street*

BOOKS

CHAPTER'S
(116 C2) (*ΩΩ F4*)
There was that Irish author who wrote that great book ... you can't remember the title? Then head on down to Chapter's. If you are looking for cheap books by fa-

mous (or not so famous) Irish writers then this will be the best place for you. The staff are exceptionally friendly and very helpful. This independent bookstore includes a large second-hand book section, where you can pick up some real finds, they also sell CDs and DVDs. *Ivy Exchange | Parnell Street | Luas Jervis*

SUB-CITY (122 C1) (*ⅢⅡ F5*)

The best comic bookshop in Ireland is not only for children. Don't be put off by the chaos: if you're looking for something in particular, the chances are the staff will be able to track it down. The shop is specialised in Irish comics, publishing many of them itself. *62 Dame Street | bus Dame Street*

SECRET BOOK & RECORD STORE (122 C2) (*ⅢⅡ G5*)

Bookworms are sure to feel at home here. You will find hardback classics for less than 5 euros, cook books and travel guides, photography books, prints and much more. And if your English isn't good enough, then go straight to the department selling cheap records and CDs. The shop is easy to miss, hence the 'secret'. *15a Wicklow Street | bus South Great George's Street*

DELICATESSEN

MAGILL'S (117 D5) (*ⅢⅡ G5*)

Delicatessen that caters to every culinary wish, the Condon family offers bread from Wicklow, cheeses and meats from all over Ireland, home-made salads, exquisite olive oil and more. *14 Clarendon Street | bus South Great George's Street*

SHERIDAN'S CHEESE SHOP ★ (117 D5) (*ⅢⅡ G5*)

Say cheese! The smell is only really seductive for real fans. Sheridan's offers

INSIDER TIP handmade specialities from Irish farms. Try the blue cheese Cashel Blue or the firm Coolea from Cork. But beware: there's a danger of buying much too much because it all tastes so good. *11 Anne Street South | bus, Luas St Stephen's Green*

FASHION & ACCESSORIES

AVOCA HANDWEAVERS ★ (117 D4) (*ⅢⅡ G5*)

The varied selection and wide range on offer makes this attractive multi-storey shop feel like a department store. Don't miss out on the *Food Hall* in the basement where you can buy all the INSIDER TIP ingredients for a lovely picnic in nearby St Stephen's Green: freshly baked bread, Irish cheeses, pies, tapas or sushi. On the ground floor there is contemporary Irish fashion and household goods. If there is no more space in the café on the top floor, simply buy the Avoca cookbook and try out the

---

★ **Powerscourt Centre**
Art, jewellery, design and a wonderfully elegant ambience
→ p. 69

★ **Temple Bar Food Market**
Delicious, healthy and organic: delicacies from the Emerald Isle
→ p. 68

★ **Avoca Handweavers**
Proof positive that contemporary Ireland has both style and taste → p. 65

★ **Sheridan's Cheese Shop**
The number of types of cheese is unbelievable! → p. 65

MARCO POLO HIGHLIGHTS

Everything is so fresh at the Temple Bar Food Market, why not ask for a taste there and then

dishes yourself. *11 Suffolk Street | bus Dame Street*

BROWN THOMAS (117 D5) (*M G5*)
This exclusive department store has four floors of fashion for men and women. On the ground floor are brands like Gucci, Hermès, Dior and Prada, and the perfume and cosmetics section has absolutely everything the heart desires. *88–95 Grafton Street | bus, Luas St Stephen's Green*

INSIDER TIP COVET – THE BORROWERS BOUDOIR (117 D5) (*M G5*)
It's all in the name and who hasn't coveted something that belongs to someone else? In this shop you can give into temptation with impunity. When you shop here you don't have to actually buy the latest ladies' fashion by international designers like Galliano or Cavalli, instead you can simply hire items – at a fraction (well, at 10 per cent) of the original price. *Powerscourt Centre | 59 William Street South | bus Dame Street*

THE FEATHERED MILLINER (116 C3) (*M F5*)
Many female Dubliners make their own hats and this shop sells hats and everything that is required for hat-making: feathers, ribbons, silk bands, millinery wire and much more. The shop is an offshoot of the neighbouring *Beads and Bling,* where you can get all the stuff you need to make your own jewellery. *34 Wellington Quay | Luas Abbey Street*

KENNEDY AND MCSHARRY (117 D5) (*M G5*)
Established in 1890, this has been Dublin's leading menswear store ever

since. The fourth generation family business sells woollen hats and caps – the kind that an Irish gentleman would wear – conservative but stylish. In addition, they also have a great selection of raincoats, tweed jackets and shirts. *Powerscourt Centre | William Street South | bus Georges Street*

LUCY'S LOUNGE
(122 C1) (*Ø F–G5*)

In this fun shop, second-hand clothes and accessories, such as skirts, trousers, jewellery, bags etc., are all sorted according to colour or a particular era. That's if you can even find it: the shop is a basement in the middle of the entertainment district. *Daily | 11 Fowner Street | bus Dame Street*

INSIDER TIP ► THE WALDORF BARBERS
(117 D3) (*Ø G5*)

An insider tip for men who want to plunge into the nightlife of Temple Bar with a decent haircut and shave – and even more exclusive as it's slightly hidden in a basement. There has been a men's barbers here since 1941. The Waldorf Barbers is based on the New York barber shops of the 1920s, the founder used to work in Waldorf Hotel in Manhattan. The pleasure doesn't come cheap – be prepared to pay 30 euros for a haircut. *13 Westmoreland Street | www.facebook.com/Waldorf.Barbershop | bus O'Connell Street, Trinity College*

FLOWERS

APPASSIONATA
(116 C5) (*Ø G5*)

You've met some nice locals and have been invited to dinner? You'll find a worthy present for your hosts at the entrance to the market hall in what is probably the most colourful and imaginative flower shop in the whole of Ireland, with its huge selection of potted plants – some planted in welly boots or watering cans. You're sure to be invited back. *Drury Street | bus South Great George's Street*

JEWELLERY

DJINN JEWELLERY
(122 C2–3) (*Ø F6*)

Djinn is no normal jewellers – it's enchanting. Simon, the owner, travels to India once a year to buy old odds and ends, which he brings back to Dublin to turn into extraordinary, unique pieces of jewellery. They are reasonably priced and you will find plenty of kitsch too – for example Jesus cufflinks. The unmistakable scent of joss sticks hangs in the air. *15a Wexford Street | Bus Wexford Street*

LOW BUDGET

Second-hand books, CDs, clothing and more can always be found in the local ❖ charity shops, several of them are in the area in and around Capel Street while second-hand books can be found at *Oxfam Books* (116 B4) (*Ø F5*) *(23 Parliament Street)*.

There is also the weekend market in the suburb of *Blackrock* (125 E5) (*Ø 0*) *(Main Street | Sat/Sun 11am–5.30pm | DART Blackrock)* on the coast south of the city. Not everything is cheap, but if you hunt around you will find some bargains: clothing, accessories, furniture and esoteric bric-a-brac.

MARKETS

HONEST2GOODNESS MARKET ⊛
(120 A2) (⬛ E2)

It is situated in an inconspicuous old warehouse facility, only a few minutes away from the Glasnevin Cemetery. On offer is mostly organic Irish produce like bread, fruit and vegetables, cheese and meat, but also olive oils, Mediterranean antipasti, organic wines and home-made curry sauces. At lunchtime there are also cooking presentations. If you'd like to make the demonstrated dish, of course all the ingredients are right on hand here. *Sat 9.30am–4pm | Glasnevin Industrial Estate | 136a Slaney Close | bus 40, 40B, 40D, 140 Finglas Road/Esso filling station*

MARKET ARCADE (116 C5) (⬛ F5)

This old market hall is a veritable treasure trove of beautiful souvenirs: goldsmith's work and handicrafts are on offer, second-hand books and CDs, Asian clothing and stylish second-hand fashion. And the food stalls are top-notch. *Between South Great George's Street and Drury Street | bus South Great George's Street*

TEMPLE BAR FOOD MARKET ★ ⊛
(116 C4) (⬛ F5)

This small Saturday market has as its focus local Irish produce, much of it organic and there is an especially tempting selection of delicious fresh farmhouse cheeses, smoked fish, handmade chocolates, jams,

FOR BOOKWORMS & FILM BUFFS

Sing Street (2016) – Dublin and the sound of the 80s are the themes of this adorable musical. The plot won't take long to explain: 15-year-old Conor Lalor from a tough family background falls in love with Raphina and comes up with the brilliant idea of forming a band called Sing Street to impress her. Director John Carney, who also made 'Once', winning him an Oscar for best soundtrack in 2008, has tapped into the true sounds of Dublin once again.

Intermission (2003) – An ensemble movie, which strings together the supposed coincidences of daily life in Dublin. The result is an absurd, funny and pacy film starring Colin Farrell, Cillian Murphy and the Dublin veteran Colm Meaney, who became internationally famous for his role as Chief O'Brien in the series 'Star Trek'. Intermission won the IFTA Award in four categories, including for best director and best script.

At Swim-Two-Birds (1939) – Flann O'Brien's novel in a novel about novel writing. It may be 80 years old, but the book is still one of the best ever written in Ireland. 'Time' magazine and the 'Guardian' newspaper both agree, counting it amongst the one hundred best English-language books of the 20th century. Plans by Brendon Gleeson, highly lauded and awarded Irish actor, to make his directorial debut with a film adaptation have been ongoing for many years. His self-proclaimed obsession with the book has seen the script go through at least fourteen drafts in the process.

preserves and gourmet sausages. *Sat 10am–4.30pm | Meeting House Square | bus Temple Bar*

SHOES

INSIDER TIP ▶ **CHINA BLUE**
(116 C3) (*ᗰ G5*)
Under the *Merchants Arch*, at the entrance to Temple Bar on the Liffey riverbank, is where you will find this shoe shop selling every make and brand from Gola, Caterpillar, Ben Sherman, Pepe to Converse. They have the full spectrum of styles from chunky Doc Martens to elegant Chinese silk slippers – even handmade cowboy boots from Venezuela. *14 Merchants Arch | Temple Bar | bus Ormond Quay*

SHOPPING CENTRES

DUNDRUM TOWN CENTRE
(125 E5) (*ᗰ 0*)
Yes, you are still in Dublin, even if you feel like you're in an American shopping mall, as you wander through Calvin Klein and Hugo Boss designer shops, cheap stores like Penneys and supermarkets. You could, in fact, spend a whole holiday in Dundrum Town Centre. The little ones would be happily occupied with the slides and jungle gym of the soft-play centre and Monday is cinema day! *Sandyford Road | Luas Dundrum*

POWERSCOURT CENTRE ⭐
(117 D5) (*ᗰ G5*)
An 18th-century aristocratic city residence has been converted into a sophisticated and exclusive shopping area selling interesting items and antiques such as clocks, silver or porcelain figurines, ball and wedding gowns, shoes and toys. The *Pygmalion Café* in the covered courtyard is the ideal place to take a rest from your shopping and to sit back and enjoy a cup of coffee and a slice of cake or a light lunch. *59 William Street South | bus Dame Street*

WHISKEY

CELTIC WHISKEY SHOP & WINES ON THE GREEN
(117 D5) (*ᗰ G5*)
A Mecca for whisk(e)y enthusiasts: nowhere in Ireland will you find a more comprehensive selection of Irish whiskey and Scottish whisky than in this award-winning store. If you're looking to buy a rare drop, then you're in the right place. However you're better off leaving the common brands well alone: they'll cost you half as much at home. Once a month there is a whiskey-tasting event. For an annual membership fee of 60 euros (overseas members 70 euros) members of Whiskey Club receive a sample of a new whiskey every two months as well as information from the world of this distinguished tipple. *27–28 Dawson Street | www.celticwhiskeyshop.com | bus St Stephen's Green North*

TEELING WHISKEY DISTILLERY
(122 B2) (*ᗰ F5*)
The only whiskey distillery in Dublin. Reason enough to drop by and maybe even take part in a guided tour. They specialise in one-offs and rarities here, for example a 33-year-old single malt of which only 275 bottles were produced – they of course carry a price tag that you may find harder to savour than the whiskey itself. You can get a mini hip flask engraved with the Teeling logo, on the other hand, for a trifling 5 euros. Book your summer visit in advance. *Daily 10am–5.40pm | tour price: 15, 20 or 30 euros, depending on how many whiskeys you want to try | 13–17 Newmarket | reservations@teeling whiskey.com | bus Patrick Street*

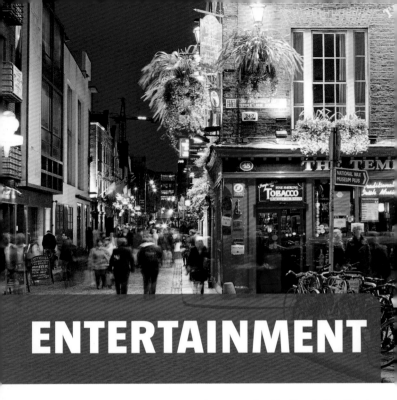

ENTERTAINMENT

CITY WHERE TO START?
(116 C4) (*∅* F–G5) Temple
Bar: This is where most bars, pubs, restaurants and night clubs are concentrated. The area between the Liffey and Dame Street, with its cobblestoned alleyways, may be geared to tourists, but is also a firm favourite with locals and Dublin's youth. *Bus An Lár | Luas Jervis*

For many, the nightlife and music scene are the main reason for visiting Dublin. Whether you like traditional Irish music in a typical old pub or prefer stylish designer bars or clubs where you can while the night away to the latest sounds: this vibrant city will not disappoint, no matter how high your expectations are.

Who knows how many pubs Dublin has? 500? 1000? In fact, it's exactly 750. That's more than enough to cater to everyone's taste, and enough to warrant a little guidance. Temple Bar is not quite as trendy as the scene in the narrow alleys south of Dame Street, around Dame Lane and Exchequer Street, while over on the north of the Liffey, on and around Ormond Quay, theme pubs attract a young clientele. The omnipresent bouncers in both areas are there to keep out those who have had too much to drink or – in the smarter clubs – those who are inappropriately dressed. This of course does not apply to pubs. Traditional pubs are scat-

Party through the night, give Guinness another chance or go to the theatre, but don't go to bed

tered across the entire inner city, especially around Merrion Row and Lower Baggot Street. As Dubin is a cultural and literary city, which has produced three Nobel Prize for Literature winners, an evening at the theatre is also highly recommended. And of course there's always a concert, whether it be Irish folk music, jazz or rock. Tickets are available at *Ticketmaster | tel. 00353 8 18 90 30 01 (*) (from outside Ireland) or 08 18 90 30 01 (*) (in Dublin) | www.ticketmaster.ie* or directly at the *Tourist Office* in Suffolk Street. Find

out what evening events are on in the free, bi-monthly 'Event Guide' *(www.entertainment.ie)*, online at *www.totally dublin.ie* and and in the bi-weekly music magazine 'Hot Press'.

BARS & CLUBS

INSIDER TIP **CHELSEA DRUGSTORE**
(122 C2) *(⬚ F5)*

At the start of the 1900s this was a pharmacy, where Messrs. Whisby sold cocoa beans to which they attributed healing powers. Today hipsters sip on cocktails here. Side effects? Relaxation! They serve small dishes and snacks too. *Daily from 4pm | 25 South Great George's Street | www.thechelseadrugstore.ie | bus South Great George's Street*

The Brazen Head: said to be Ireland's oldest pub

INSIDER TIP THE LIQUOR ROOMS
(116 C4) (*ω F5*)

This cocktail bar is the only one in Ireland nominated for the Tales of the Cocktail Spirited Awards. If you think you've got the casual shake of a born bartender, then the cocktail course (30 euros) is the thing for you. Otherwise take part in a whiskey tasting for the same price and meet at least six other enthusiasts searching for high-proof esprit in a snifter glass. You'll even receive a welcome present. If you don't want to drink on an

empty stomach, order a mixed plate of starters for 11 to 15 euros. The Prosecco punch is ready to go for 150 euros, if you have something to celebrate and can put away approx. 25 portions between you and your friends. Oh yes: there are music events too. *Daily | 5pm to late | 5 Wellington Quay | tel. 08 73 39 36 88 | www.theliquorrooms.com | bus Wellington Quay*

OPIUM ROOMS
(122 C3) (*ω F6*)

All good things (including bar rooms) come in threes: music events regularly take place in the main space, with its excellent acoustics and light show – Run The Jewels, Groove Armada, Mount Kimbie, Kiasmos and Pantha Du Prince and many others have performed here. Fans of fresh air go to the garden with its heated terrace and dance floor. Smokers like to congregate on the terrace of the small lounge, with its own bar. There's also a restaurant (*Moderate*), where fans of Asian food are sure to find what they are looking for. INSIDER TIP Earlybird dinner from 5 to 7pm at a discount. *Mon–Wed midday–10pm, Thu/Fri midday–11pm, Sat 1pm–11pm, Sun 1pm–10pm | 26 Wexford Street | www.opiumrooms.ie | bus Camden Street*

BINGO

● Bingo is played more passionately in Ireland than anywhere else – especially by women. The game callers have their own bingo 'lingo' with names for the numbers, like 'two little ducks' for 22, so it's a real experience attending a game. Bingo evenings take place in the community halls or at the *National Stadium*. (*Tue, Thu and Sun | South Circular Road | www.nationalstadiumbingo.com | bus 68, 122 South Circular Road*). It was introduced by the Catholic Church, who used the profits for the upkeep of the church building.

CINEMA

INSIDER TIP IRISH FILM INSTITUTE ●
(116 C4) *(ₘ F5)*

If you are looking for a sophisticated art house film, you should head for the Irish Film Institute (IFI). It also hosts an annual international film festival. The institute shows classics, short and documentary films and new independent Irish films and releases from all around the world, making you hope that it will continue to rain for a little longer. During the day the restaurant is an ideal place for a simple meal at reasonable prices. Alongside it is a well stocked film bookshop with a huge selection of Irish DVDs. The sun is shining again? Who cares! *6 Eustace Street | tel. 016 79 34 77 | www. ifi.ie | bus Temple Bar*

LIGHT HOUSE CINEMA
(120 B6) *(ₘ F4)*

Shows mainly independent films. There is a café, and you are allowed to bring your own wine to drink during screenings. *Market Square Smithfield | www. lighthousecinema.ie | Luas Smithfield*

LIVE MUSIC

THE BRAZEN HEAD ★ ●
(116 A4) *(ₘ F5)*

Officially Ireland's oldest pub, The Brazen Head was apparently founded in 1198. Its medieval crenellated façade is lit with flaming torches and welcomes guests in true pub style. While the year of origin may be doubtful, it is true that there has been a tavern here since 1600. Every evening there is live traditional music in the packed hall next to the paved courtyard. *20 Lower Bridge Street | free admis-sion | tel. 016 77 95 49 | www.brazenhead. com | Luas Four Courts*

BUTTON FACTORY
(116 C4) *(ₘ F5)*

The only buttons you'll find here are the ones on the clothes of the guests and artists. The programme showcases new, innovative musicians and bands; but well-known, established stars such as Van Morrison have also performed here. *Curved Street | tel. 016 70 91 05 | www. buttonfactory.ie | bus Temple Bar*

THE COBBLESTONE ★
(120 B6) *(ₘ E4)*

The décor may leave much to be desired but good music is the real attraction here. A sign in the musicians' area next to the entrance says, 'Listening area – please

---

MARCO POLO HIGHLIGHTS

★ **The Brazen Head**
Historical atmosphere and traditional music → p. 73

★ **The Cobblestone**
Inconspicuous exterior but a leader in the music scene → p. 73

★ **The Grand Social**
Premier address for live music → p. 74

★ **Mulligan's**
A classicong the old established Dublin pubs → p. 75

★ **The Stag's Head**
An authentic pub with a beautiful 19th-century interior → p. 76

★ **Gate Theatre**
First-class theatre in an 18th-century venue → p. 77

respect musicians'. In the pub itself the atmosphere is more relaxed and music is played in INSIDERTIP *The Backroom* where new and established bands perform for large audiences. This place has an authentic Irish atmosphere, which connoisseurs of the Irish music scene will appreciate. *77 North King Street | tel. 01 8 72 17 99 | Luas Smithfield*

O'DONOGHUE'S (117 E6) (*Ø G5*)

This simple pub enjoys a legendary reputation due to the quality of the Irish music that you can hear here every evening. O'Donoghue's is best known as the birthplace of the band *The Dubliners*. Neither the fame of the pub nor the tourists that pop in here constantly have impacted on its cosy atmosphere. On warmer days the guests like to drink their Guinness at the bar tables outside. *15 Merrion Row | tel. 01 6 60 71 94 | www.odonoghues.ie | bus, Luas St Stephen's Green*

THE GRAND SOCIAL ⭐
(116 C3) (*Ø F4*)

A really very special venue! The bar has many unusual beers on tap – at the expense of some more standard brews. The club in the basement offers a range of music from rock through hip-hop to electronic. Smaller gigs take place in the upper-floor 'Loft', a room boasting interesting design and excellent acoustics. The real highlight is the spacious beer garden on the roof. Only the toilets leave a little to be desired. *35 Lower Liffey Street | tel. 01 8 74 00 76 | www.the grandsocial.ie | Luas Jervis*

HUGHES' BAR ●
(116 A3) (*Ø F5*)

A rather large pub that is not very atmospheric but what it lacks in atmosphere it makes up for with its excellent traditional Irish music sessions – one of the best

Dublin has to offer. *20 Chancery Street | Luas Four Courts*

VICAR STREET (122 B2) (*Ø F5*)

This establishment has been voted Ireland's best music venue three times. The performances span the entire music spectrum from folk and traditional music to black country, pop, blues and jazz. *8 Thomas Street | www.vicarstreet.com | bus Thomas Street*

WHELAN'S (122C3) (*Ø F6*)

A traditional pub that is also a very famous music venue that caters to all sorts: rock, indie, traditional, electronic and Irish. The Wexford Street is the epicentre of the slightly rundown *Village Quarter* area. Another trendy music venue nearby is *Anseo (28 Camden Street)*. *25 Wexford Street | tel. 01 4 78 07 66 | www.whelans live.com | Luas St Stephen's Green*

PUBS

INSIDERTIP THE BERNARD SHAW
(122 C3) (*Ø F6*)

Yes, it's a pub with craft beer – but that's not all: pizzas are sold from a blue bus in the beer garden and there's a flea market at the weekend. *Mon–Fri from 4pm, Sat 1pm–1am, Sun 1pm–11pm | 11–12 South Richmond Street | www.thebernardshaw. com | bus Richmond Street South/Lennox Street*

INSIDERTIP THE BLACK SHEEP
(120 B6) (*Ø F4*)

Here you'll find all common varieties of beer alongside ones made in the house brewery *(Galway Bay Brewery)* and at other micro-breweries – 40 on tap and at least as many again in bottles. Sometimes there are performances by comedians, and you can borrow board games for free. For lunch and dinner they serve meals which are a cut above your standard pub food, and the prices, ranging between 10 and 15 euros, are absolutely affordable. *61 Capel Street | www.galwaybaybrewery.com/blacksheep | bus Parnell Square West*

INTERNATIONAL BAR
(117 D4) (*ᗰ G5*)

The third generation family that runs this pub wants to keep its authentic Irish character and doesn't exploit its mention

MULLIGAN'S ★ ●
(117 E3) (*ᗰ G5*)

If you have a look around in this old pub, you will know why it has been an institute in Dublin for generations. Dark wood, discrete nooks and theatre posters create an atmosphere that even James Joyce and John F. Kennedy (as a young newspaper reporter) could treasure. And no one pours

An intimate chat in O'Donoghue's? You can forget it once the musicians unpack their instruments

in James Joyce's novel 'Ulysses'. The price of a Guinness here is palatable and the audience is a pleasant mix of young and old, chic and shabby. The rooms are also popular comedy and jazz venues. *23 Wicklow Street | bus Dame Street*

THE LONG HALL (122 C2) (*ᗰ F5*)

Wonderfully authentic pub where ordinary Dubliners like to meet up for a drink. The room is long and narrow with lots of mirrored glass, crystal chandeliers and

Guinness better than the crew behind this counter. *8 Poolbeg Street | DART Tara Street*

INSIDER TIP O'SHEA'S MERCHANT
(116 A4) (*ᗰ F5*)

Traditional Irish set dancing has a stronger following in the provinces than in Dublin, where the younger audience prefers international and modern dancing. However, the large pub O'Shea still likes to maintain tradition and there is a section in the back where traditional music sessions take place. The pub serves suitably hearty meals like Irish stew. *Daily | free admission | 12 Lower Bridge Street | Luas Four Courts*

THE PORTERHOUSE (116 B4) (*🗺 F5*)
This popular pub with bar counters on several floors is a stroke of luck for beer lovers. There is nothing wrong with Guinness, the black elixir of life is beyond reproach. However, this also means that Dublin has a kind of beer monoculture as the draft beer on tap in every pub is Guinness and their affiliated brands. The INSIDERTIP microbrewery *Porterhouse,* on the other hand, brews their own excellent quality beer. Try *Porterhouse Red, Plain, Oyster Stout* or their *Templebräu* pilsner which is brewed with German hops, best paired with some classic pub

fare. At the weekend there's live music to round off the whole experience. *16–18 Parliament Street | bus Temple Bar*

THE STAG'S HEAD ⭐
(116 C4) (*🗺 G5*)
The interior of this Victorian pub is well worth seeing: stained glass windows, a mounted 'Stag's Head', red plush seats, dark wood, old mirrors and marble topped tables. At weekends, this pub, hidden in a small alleyway between Trinity Street and South Great George's Street, is packed and there is live music in the basement and an additional bar on the first floor. *1 Dame Court | bus Dame Street*

DANCE, THEATRE & SHOWS

ABBEY THEATRE (117 D2) (*🗺 G4*)
Since its foundation in 1904, the Abbey Theatre has a prominent place in the cultural life of this literature-obsessed country. The stage encouraged a generation of Irish to produce a body of literary work now known as the Irish Literary Revival, to whom Ireland's first Nobel laureate, William Butler Yeats, also belonged. Riots broke out during the premiere performance of the 'shocking' new work, Sean O'Casey's 'The Plough and the Stars', because the public felt that the left-wing dramatist had not treated Ireland's rebel history with enough respect. In 1951 the song 'Keep the Home Fires Burning' played at the closing of the performance, then the theatre burned down. It was only in 1966 that it was rebuilt. At the reopening, 'The Plough and the Stars' was once again performed – this time around without any scandal. Today the Abbey is well known for its excellent productions. The smaller studio stage *The Peacock* dedicates itself mostly to the works of new dramatists. *26 Lower Abbey Street | tickets Mon–Sat 10.30am–*

LOW BUDGET

The beer on the outskirts of the city may be cheaper, but in many city centre pubs there is also ● live music – without having to pay an admission fee. Good options: *The Brazen Head (20 Lower Bridge Street), Oliver St John Gogarty (58–59 Fleet Street)* and especially *Hughes' Bar (20 Chancery Street | Luas Four Courts),* where you can also often hear bagpipes being played.

The film 'Once', awarded an Oscar for its soundtrack, is a tribute to the *buskers* on Grafton Street. At weekends, a dozen street musicians vie for attention. Quality varies, but many are well worth a listen. Don't forget to throw a few coins in the hat.

7pm | tel. 01 8 78 72 22 | www.abbeythea tre.ie | Luas Abbey Street

BORD GÁIS ENERGY THEATRE (FORMER GRAND CANAL THEATRE)
(123 E1) (*M* H5)

Stand in front of the Grand Canal just before a theatre evening, when it is already dark, and just let the architecture take its effect. The theatre in the Docklands was designed by star architect Daniel Libeskind. It produces ballets, musicals, classic orchestra music and opera. *Grand Canal Square | tel. 0818 71 93 77 (*) | bord gaisenergytheatre.ie | DART Pearse Street/ Grand Canal Dock*

COISCÉIM

This creative modern dance ensemble (the name means 'footsteps') under the leading Irish choreographer David Bolger is a sensation both at home and internationally. Performances take place at various venues, often at *Project Arts Centre (39 Essex Street East | tickets 10am–*

6pm | tel. 01 8 81 96 13 | www.project.ie | bus Temple Bar). Info at tel. 01 8 78 05 58 | www.coisceim.com

GAIETY THEATRE (117 D5) (*M* G5)

The extravagant design of this 1871 theatre is in itself worth the visit. The productions are suitable for a wide audience: musicals, famous dramas, concerts and operas. *King Street South | tickets Mon– Sat 10am–6pm | tel. 0818 71 93 88 (*) | www.gaietytheatre.com | bus, Luas St Stephen's Green*

GATE THEATRE ★
(120 C5) (*M* G4)

This wonderful 18th-century theatre makes an excellent backdrop for performances of works by well known European and American authors, but also young Irish talents. The Gate is also an important venue for Samuel Beckett fans. *1 Cavendish Row | at Parnell Square | tickets Mon– Sat 10am–7.30pm | tel. 01 8 74 40 45 | www.gatetheatre.ie | bus O'Connell Street*

Architect Daniel Libeskind also does stages: Bord Gáis Energy Theatre

WHERE TO STAY

Even the last pub closes at some point. And then you're allowed to sleep for a couple of hours.

But where? Sleeping at the Merrion or Shelbourne Hotel is comfortable and classy. Small family hotels or bed & breakfasts are cosy, youth hostels, on the other hand, are functional, but sometimes also offer single, double or family rooms. There are, of course, more exclusive options: how about booking a couple of nights in the house of former Formula 1 driver Eddie Irvine? It's possible via online portals such as Airbnb. Beds for ten people, sauna, whirlpool, games room and a wonderful view across Dublin Bay from Dalkey don't come cheap though. But maybe one of the neighbours, Bono, The Edge or Van Morrison,

will call round to borrow a cup of sugar. Wouldn't that alone be worth the 1200 euros a night?

By the way, a rare edition of 'Et Tu Healy', the first published poem by James Joyce, who was nine years old at the time, would cost you exactly the same amount. Ok, so that's not going to help you book your accommodation in Dublin. But you could rent the converted garden house in Blackrock *(short.travel/ dbl9)* where Joyce wrote this poem for 100 euros a night.

Much more important than celebrities, alive or dead, is the question of what you plan to do in Dublin: if the focus of your Dublin visit is more on the nightlife, then you should stay in the centre of town. But if you are looking for a more natural out-

Dublin may never sleep but you will certainly need to ... and some comfortable accommodation is always welcome

door environment and fresh air to relax after a sightseeing (or shopping) tour in Dublin, then a better bet for you would be the suburbs on the coast or at Phoenix Park, where there are a number of suitable options.

Just as important as a good night's sleep is the question of setting yourself up properly for the day with a good breakfast. Big hotels almost always serve a warm breakfast buffet, so you can pick and choose to create your own meal (though it's not always included). Other-

wise you may be offered a continental breakfast, with bread rolls, toast and pastries and a selection of sweet and savoury toppings and preserves. For peak season you should book your accommodation in Dublin long in advance, otherwise you may end up out on the street – especially if your visit happens to coincide with an important sporting event or big rock concert.

The official tourist information *Dublin Tourism (www.visitdublin.com)* offers an excellent accommodation service including online bookings. Keep an eye out for specials and last-minute deals. It is also possible to get advice and make bookings by telephone or directly at the offices of *Dublin Tourism* at the airport and in the city centre.

HOTELS: EXPENSIVE

CLARENCE HOTEL ⭐ (116 C3) (*🛱 G5*)

U2 musicians Bono and Edge liked this venerable old hotel in the Temple Bar so much that they bought it and re-developed it into a chic boutique hotel. The rooms are individually furnished, the bathrooms are the epitome of quality and luxury. Double rooms with a view onto the Liffey over 300 euros. *44 rooms. | 6–8 Wellington Quay | tel. 01 40 70 80 00 | www.theclarence.ie | bus Temple Bar*

THE DYLAN ⭐ (123 E3) (*🛱 H6*)

The fine boutique hotel's location in the green residential area south of the Grand Canal couldn't be much better for shopping and sightseeing: from here you can reach everything quickly by foot. If you still aren't tired after all that, go to the hotel's private fitness centre. You can even bring your pets, as long as they behave themselves. And if you've already done enough walking, there's a dog walker to take care of Fido's needs. *44 rooms | Eastmoreland Place | tel. 01 6 60 30 00 | www.dylan.ie | DART Grand Canal Quay | 10 min walk*

THE GIBSON HOTEL

(121 F6) (*🛱 J4*)

The hotel prides itself on being an oasis of calm in the bustling inner city. The spectacular building is flooded with natural light, and there is something for every purse, from family room to pent-house suite. The rooms boast beds that are kind to your back with strip lighting underneath, and wi-fi and use of the fitness centre is included in the price. From the heated terrace of the 🍃 *BBQ Grill*

Don't start counting the windows at The Marker or your'll never get to bed

on the sixth floor you have a great view over the Docklands and the Liffey. *251 rooms | Point Village | tel. 01 68 15 00 00 | www.thegibsonhotel.ie | Luas The Point*

THE MARKER HOTEL ☼
(123 E1) *(𝄞 H5)*

Luxury joint with a roof terrace, offering views of the Dublin Mountains – and the sea of course. Swim a few lengths of the infinity pool or sweat it all out in the sauna, before relaxing at the cocktail bar. Physics nerds will enjoy the unique geometric design of the hotel, which was inspired by something like the columns of the Giant's Causeway. *187 rooms | Grand Canal Square | tel. 01 6 87 51 00 | www. themarkerhoteldublin.com | DART Pearse Street/Grand Canal Dock*

NUMBER 31
(123 D3) *(𝄞 G6)*

Run by a married couple, the Comers, this Georgian house on Fitzwilliam Place (and a modern extension on Leeson Close) lies in one of the most elegant suburbs of Dublin. All rooms en suite and are individually decorated, breakfast is served in a wonderful conservatory. *21 rooms | 31 Leeson Close | tel. 01 6 76 50 11 | www.number31.ie | bus Leeson Street Lower | Aircoach Leeson Street Lower*

RIU PLAZA THE GRESHAM HOTEL
(117 D1) *(𝄞 G4)*

A place for discerning travellers to Dublin since 1817. Comprehensively renovated, the imposing façade and the large lobby now live up to their promise. If you can't afford to stay overnight, but don't want to miss out on its elegant style, just pop in for a delicious afternoon tea between 2pm and 6pm. *284 rooms | 23 O'Connell Street Upper | tel. 01 8 74 68 81 | www. gresham-hotels.com | Aircoach O'Connell Street | airport bus 747*

THE SHELBOURNE
(117 D6) *(𝄞 G5)*

A true Dublin institute. The heritage rooms in the old wing maintain the elegance of a bygone era. A little less expensive, but still very luxurious, are the rooms in the modern wing. Afternoon tea in the *Lord Mayor's Lounge* is a real experience and you will find celebrities at the ● *Horseshoe Bar*, while in the INSIDER TIP *Oyster Bar* high society meets to eat oysters and drink champagne. *265 rooms | 27 St Stephen's Green | tel. 01 6 63 45 00 | www.marriott. com | Aircoach St Stephen's Green*

HOTELS: MODERATE

ARIEL HOUSE ★
(123 F3) *(𝄞 J6)*

Ambassadors from many countries appreciate the peace and quiet in affluent Ballsbridge, southeast of the city centre. If it's good enough for diplomats, is good enough for you: The hotel is in a stylish 19th-century house and has been fur-

---

MARCO POLO HIGHLIGHTS

★ **The Dylan**
Dublin's only boutique hotel with five stars → p. 80

★ **Harrington Hall**
Welcoming Georgian hotel that was once a hostel run by nuns → p. 83

★ **Clarence Hotel**
Just the way U2 like it: luxury and style directly on the river → p. 80

★ **Trinity College**
Live where others study: rooms in the 400-year-old university → p. 85

nished with an eye for detail and many antiques. What's more, the best: The city centre is within easy walking distance. *37 rooms | 50–54 Lansdowne Road | tel. 01 6 68 55 12 | www.arielhouse.net | DART Lansdowne Road*

BUSWELL'S HOTEL (117 E5) *(𝄞 G5)*
Buswell's Hotel may not be very fashionable but its location – in the middle of the city and near all the best shopping areas – makes it a good choice. The Georgian architecture of its three historic townhouses is matched by its classic dark wooden furniture and décor. Guests can use the secure parking and eat and drink in the comfortable *Buswell's Bar. 67 rooms | 23–27 Molesworth Street | tel. 01 6 14 65 00 | www.buswells.ie | bus Merrion Square | Aircoach Merrion Square*

THE CENTRAL (116 C4) *(𝄞 F5)*
Established in 1887, this is one of the oldest hotels in Dublin, but the rooms are

MORE THAN A GOOD NIGHT'S SLEEP

Elegant and in the thick of it
You'd rather be out in the hustle and bustle of Dublin than sleep? You can combine both at *The Morgan* **(117 D3)** *(𝄞 G5)* *(121 rooms | 10–12 Fleet Street | tel. 01 6 43 70 00 | www.themorgan. com | Bus An Lár/City Centre | Moderate–Expensive)* The four-star boutique hotel is right in the middle of the entertainment district Temple Bar. Refuel for the long night ahead in the hotel's own fitness room, in the cocktail bar or on the rooftop garden.

Snooze through school
You can now lay your head to rest where school desks once served as barricades and bullet holes from the Easter Rising distracted pupils till the early 1960s. There's also a restaurant and bar in the former classrooms of the *Schoolhouse Hotel* **(123 E2)** *(𝄞 H6)* *(31 rooms | 2–8 Northumberland Road | tel. 01 6 67 50 14 | www.schoolhouse hotel.com | DART Grand Canal Dock | Moderate)*, a school building from 1861. Aviva Stadium and Bord Gais Energy Theatre are around the corner.

Cheap and trendy
Cheap, central, no frills, that's the award-winning INSIDER TIP *The Generator Hostel* **(116 A3)** *(𝄞 F4)* *(106 rooms | 28 Smithfield Street | tel. 01 9 01 02 22 | generatorhostels.com | Luas Smithfield | Budget–Expensive)* on trendy Smithfield Market. In fact, it's everything you need to take on the city. A bed in an eight-bed room costs 14 euros, your own room with three beds and bathroom 170 euros. There are also rooms with whirlpool, a restaurant and a lounge bar.

Room with a view
If you want to unwind from the hustle and bustle of the big city, the bed and breakfast ✹ *Dalkey Island View* **(125 F5)** *(𝄞 0)* *(4 rooms | tel. 08 60 65 11 90 | DART Dalkey | Moderate)*, a pink Georgian house with Victorian furniture in the well-to-do suburb of Dalkey, is the right place for you. Breakfast is served on the balcony with a view of Killiney Bay – if the weather allows. But sitting in the kitchen is wonderful too, where the roaring fireplace will help you forget the rain.

Retro isn't just a word at Dean Dublin

very modern and offer everything you can expect from a three-star hotel. In its *Library Bar* with all its old books, time seems to have come to a stand still. *70 rooms | 1–5 Exchequer Street | tel. 01 6 79 73 02 | www.centralhoteldublin.com | bus Dame Street/South Great George's Street*

INSIDER TIP ▶ DEAN DUBLIN
(122 C3) (𝄞 G6)

Hipsters love all of that cool stuff, like modern Irish art, Marshall amps for their gadgets, vinyl for the retro record collection. So does the Dean Dublin. The restaurant serves cocktails and decent food, but the highlight is 'Highline', from 11pm, Thursday to Saturday, on the rooftop terrace Sophie's on the Roof. You'll feel like you're in New York (you'll have to go to find out more!). You're also welcome to join the party if you aren't stay-

ing at the Dean. By the way, every trip to the toilet here is good for your ecological conscience: it's flushed using 🌿 pure rain water. *52 rooms | 33 Harcourt Street | Saint Kevin's | tel. 01 6 07 81 10 | deandublin.ie | bus Harcourt Street | Luas St Stephen's Green (10 min walk)*

HARRINGTON HALL ★
(122 C3) (𝄞 G6)

Nuns once watched over the young women who they accommodated here. Today the family-run hall near St Stephan's Green, renovated in blue and yellow tones, is open to everyone. Free parking and a good breakfast are also available. Ask for INSIDER TIP ▶ a room on the first floor – the windows are larger and the view on to the streets better. *28 rooms | 70 Harcourt Street | tel. 01 4 75 34 97 | www.harringtonhall.com | Luas Harcourt*

KELLY'S HOTEL

(116 C5) (*∅ F5*)

The hotel above *Hogan's Bar* is sparsely furnished but nonetheless offers everything you need and the French cuisine hotel restaurant, *L'Gueuleton,* is considered to be one of the best places to eat out in Dublin. And its *Secret Bar* is famous for its mojitos. *16 rooms | 36 South Great George's Street | tel. 01 6 48 00 10 | www.kellysdublin.com | bus South Great George's Street*

TEMPLE BAR HOTEL

(117 D3) (*∅ G5*)

A modern hotel in the centre of the city's entertainment district, which means that it can get rather loud. The 129 rooms have modern furnishings and Internet is free. Look out for their special offers, e.g. three nights for the price of two. Its bright conservatory-style *Terrace Restaurant* is decorated with contemporary art. *43–45 Fleet Street | tel. 01 6 77 33 33 | www. templebarhotel.com | bus Fleet Street/ Westmoreland Street*

LOW BUDGET

If you want to party and then fall into bed, your best bet is the backpacker hostel *Barnacles (19 Temple Lane South | tel. 01 6 71 62 77 | www.bar nacles.ie)* in the middle of the bustling Temple Bar district. The hostel is clean and safe and its rooms are bright. Double rooms available from 30 euros, in the communal rooms you pay as little as 12 euros a night.

Mercer Court (Lower Mercer Street | tel. 01 2 78 80 93 | www.dublin-hotels.net/mercer-court | bus, Luas St Stephen's Green) is a student hall that rents out 100 en-suite rooms to visitors during the holidays between the end of June and September – cheaper than Trinity College and often of a better standard. Single rooms from 60 euros, double rooms from 90 euros.

INSIDER TIP ▶ **ABC GUESTHOUSE**

(121 D2) (*∅ G2*)

A friendly reception and a generous breakfast await visitors to this reasonably priced bed and breakfast in the north of Dublin. It is right on the bus route between the airport and the inner city. *3 rooms | 57 Drumcondra Road Upper | tel. 01 8 36 74 17 | www.abchousedublin. com | bus from airport 16A, 41, 746 Skylon Hotel*

BERESFORD HOTEL

(117 E2) (*∅ G4*)

Located close to the bus station, the hotel used to be a wine store. The in-house restaurant *Il Vignardo* has an extended 'Happy Hour' when prices are low. *103 rooms | Store Street | tel. 01 8 13 47 00 | www.beresfordhotelifsc.com | bus Busáras | DART Connolly Station | Luas Connolly Station*

PHOENIX PARK HOTEL

(119 F5) (*∅ E4*)

For everyone who enjoys a breath of fresh air or some exercise in the big city, Phoenix Park is right on the doorstep. Their single, double and family rooms are all en suite and tastefully furnished, and the excellent breakfast is also available as a vegetarian option. Conveniently situated near Heuston Station. *29 rooms | 38–39 Parkgate Street | tel. 01 6 77 28 70 | www. phoenixparkhotel.ie | Luas Heuston*

HOSTELS & STUDENT ACCOMMODATION

INSIDER TIP ▸ AVALON HOUSE
(116 C6) (ℳ F5)

It almost sounds too good to be true: a night in the heart of Dublin from 10 euros? And breakfast is included too! Single, double, four-bed and shared rooms are available and you can use the kitchen and lockers for free. There's even access to the Internet into the bargain. You haven't got a computer with you? No problem: the hostel will provide you with one of those too at no extra cost. Book in advance! *281 beds | 55 Aungier Street | tel. 014 75 00 01 | www.avalon-house.ie | bus 16 from airport*

TRINITY COLLEGE ★
(117 D4) (ℳ G5)

During the semester holidays, from June to September, the university rents out historical and modern student rooms to tourists. The accommodation is quite acceptable and the characters of the rooms vary. Many have a beautiful view on to the old courtyards of the college and about half of them have their own bathrooms. There are also double rooms and small apartments with kitchens. Bed and breakfast 60 euros/person. *600 rooms | Trinity College | tel. 018 96 44 77 | www.tcd.ie/accommodation/Visitors | bus Aircoach Grafton Street*

APARTMENTS

OLIVER ST JOHN GOGARTY PENTHOUSE APARTMENTS ☼
(117 D3) (ℳ G5)

These apartments are on the fifth floor above the pub *Oliver St John Gogarty* and are in the middle of the Temple Bar entertainment district. Despite their location they are very quiet and a great alternative to an expensive hotel in the city centre for a INSIDER TIP ▸ family vacation. Five of the apartments have two bedrooms that sleep a maximum of four persons, a further apartment offers three bedrooms for six people, and all contain a living and dining room as well as kitchen. The view over the roofs of Dublin is astounding, the central location unbeatable and the price *(apartment for 4 Sun–Thu 99 euros/night in the off-season, 119 euros/night in peak season, Fri/Sat*

Trinity College: sleep where the think tanks of the future incubate

149 in the off-season, 199 euros/night in peak season; apartment for 6 Sun–Thu 129 euros/night in the off-season, 149 euros/night in peak season, Fri/Sat 195 euros/night in the off-season, 249 euros/night in peak season) reasonable. *6 apts. | 18–21 Anglesea Street | tel. 016 71 18 22 | www.gogartys.ie | bus Grafton Street | Aircoach Grafton Street*

DISCOVERY TOURS

① DUBLIN AT A GLANCE

START: ① Bewley's Café
END: ⑭ Temple Bar

1 day
Actual walking time
2½ hours

Distance:
🔁 22 km/13.7 mi (7 km/4.35 mi on foot)

COSTS: 75 euros/pers. for breakfast, picnic, evening meal, bicycle hire and admission fees (❻ St Michan's Church 5 euros, ❸ Book of Kells 10 euros, ❿ Kilmainham Gaol 9 euros)

IMPORTANT TIPS: ❸ Book of Kells: Long waiting times in high season
❻ St Michan's Church: Note opening times of the vaults
❿ Kilmainham Gaol: Book in advance; often crowded

In terms of surface area, Dublin is large, but the inner city is compact and easy to cover on foot. Take this day tour to give you a good first glance at the most important attractions Dublin has to offer. But uncover a few seemingly not-so-

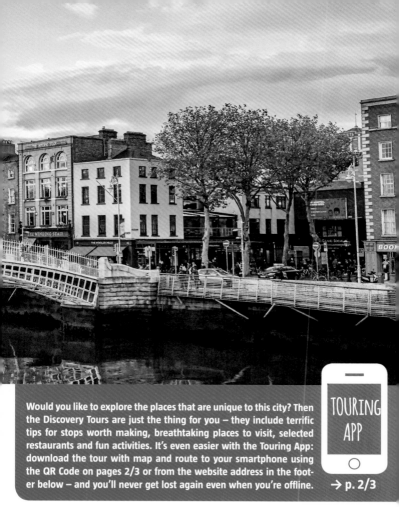

Would you like to explore the places that are unique to this city? Then the Discovery Tours are just the thing for you – they include terrific tips for stops worth making, breathtaking places to visit, selected restaurants and fun activities. It's even easier with the Touring App: download the tour with map and route to your smartphone using the QR Code on pages 2/3 or from the website address in the footer below – and you'll never get lost again even when you're offline.

TOURING APP

○

→ p. 2/3

important details, too, which are just as exciting and feature among the many facets of the Irish capital.

09:00am The walk begins with breakfast at **❶ Bewley's Café** → **p. 54 in Grafton Street**. Ernest Bewley opened the café in 1927, taking his inspiration from the Viennese coffee houses and oriental tea rooms of the day. Bewley's has been CO_2-neutral since 2008 and serves up many organic products. Give the organic porridge or the sweet pancakes a try.

❶ Bewley's Café

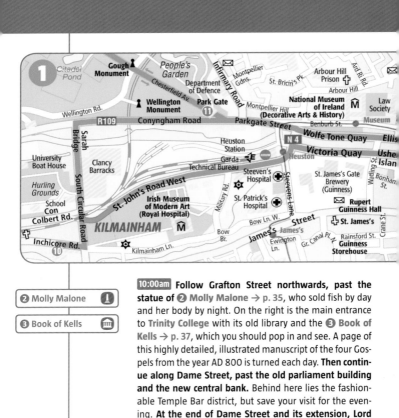

② Molly Malone 🎵

③ Book of Kells 🏛

④ Christ Church Cathedral 🏠

⑤ Leo Burdock 🍴

10:00am Follow Grafton Street northwards, past the statue of **②** **Molly Malone** → p. 35, who sold fish by day and her body by night. On the right is the main entrance to **Trinity College** with its old library and the **③** **Book of Kells** → p. 37, which you should pop in and see. A page of this highly detailed, illustrated manuscript of the four Gospels from the year AD 800 is turned each day. **Then continue along Dame Street, past the old parliament building and the new central bank.** Behind here lies the fashionable Temple Bar district, but save your visit for the evening. **At the end of Dame Street and its extension, Lord Edward Street,** take a quick look inside the early Gothic **④** **Christ Church Cathedral** → p. 38, one of two Protestant cathedrals in Dublin. Note the glass cabinet in the crypt, which contains the mummified rat and cat found inside an organ pipe.

12:00pm Hungry again already? **Opposite the cathedral, at the top of Werburgh Street, is ⑤ Leo Burdock** → p. 61, the most famous 'chipper' in Ireland. The likes of Mick Jagger, Liam Neeson, Rod Stewart, Tom Cruise, Bruce Springsteen and even Edith Piaf got their hands greasy on a portion of fish and chips here. **Suitably fortified, your route continues along Bridge Street, past Dublinia → p. 41 and St Audoen's Church,** which was built for Polish Catholics in the 12th century. **At the end, shortly before the Liffey,** stands Dublin's oldest public house, The Brazen Head → p. 73, with its sloping walls and gunshot holes

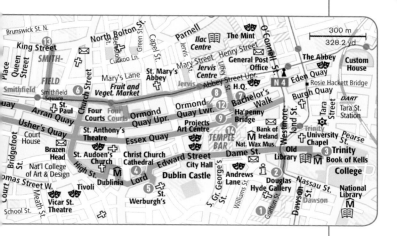

left over from the Easter Rising of 1916; it's too early for a pint, though. **Carry on across Father Mathew Bridge, passing the Four Courts on the left, and walk along Church Street as far as ⑥ St Michan's Church → p. 46.** It's worth stopping off here. It is said that Handel played his Messias here at the keyboard of the organ in the foyer. In the vaults underneath the church there are chambers full of corpses, many of which have been lying here for five hundred or, in some cases, eight hundred years. The tannin level in the air has prevented their decomposure. It's hardly surprising therefore that Bram Stoker found his inspiration for his Dracula down here.

02:00pm After that, retrace your steps a little and turn left into Chancery Street. This will take you to Abbey Street, past the Victorian Dublin Corporation Fruit and Vegetable Market built in 1892. Leaving aside the Leprechaun Museum → p. 103, which devotes its attention entirely to the sprite from Irish folklore, **continue down Abbey Street and turn right into Liffey Street.** On the right is ⑦ **The Bakehouse** *(6 Bachelors Walk | daily)*, a bakery that upholds the traditional craft. Buy some sweet and savoury baked goods and pack them in your rucksack – for later. **The route continues along Liffey Street down to the river Liffey. Once there, turn right and then right again between La Taverna and Bar Italia into the tiny alleyway known as Bloom Lane.** Take a look at ⑧ **Dublin's Last Supper** → p. 43 by artist John Byrne, who used this Irish

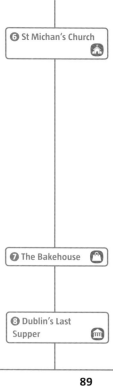

⑥ St Michan's Church

⑦ The Bakehouse

⑧ Dublin's Last Supper

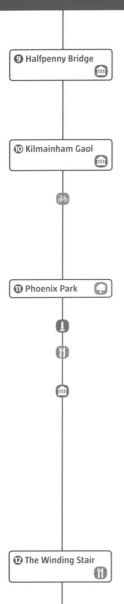

⑨ Halfpenny Bridge

⑩ Kilmainham Gaol

⑪ Phoenix Park

⑫ The Winding Stair

take on da Vinci's masterpiece to illustrate the changes in Irish society. **Go back again and cross over the cast-iron ⑨ Halfpenny Bridge →** p. 35 **and, turning left, walk along the other side of the Liffey as far as the corner of Westmoreland Street.**

03:00pm **Hop onto bus No. 69 (towards Rathcoole) at stop 4720 and ride as far as stop 2640 (Inchicore Road/Kilmainham Jail).** From here it's just 30 m (33 yd) to the entrance of ⑩ **Kilmainham Gaol →** p. 50. A guided tour of the old prison is like a crash course in Irish history, as it was here that Ireland's rebels were imprisoned from 1796 until its closure in 1924. Don't forget to visit the **Prison Museum**. Next, hire yourself a bicycle – you'll find a branch of **Dublin Bikes →** p. 112 in front of the prison. **Cycle to the right along Inchicore Road and turn left into South Circular Road. Cross the Liffey and at the end of the road turn right into Conyngham Road and the short stretch as far as Parkgate Street.**

05:00pm Turn off into the main entrance of ⑪ **Phoenix Park →** p. 50, the largest urban park in Europe, which is home to the Irish president, the American ambassador and any number of fallow deer. **Head for the Wellington-Monument**, the obelisk to your left, and take your high-tea picnic there, the ingredients for which you bought earlier at Ichiman. After you've had your picnic, cycle up **Chesterfield Avenue until just before the roundabout.** Take a peek to the right through the fence at the presidential palace. Follow the track around **in a northeasterly direction along North Road, then turn right and continue along Spa Road and Polo Road past the All Ireland Polo Club and back onto Chesterfield Avenue. Carry on down to the park gate, at which point** you can return your bicycle on the opposite side of the road on Parkgate Street. **Retrace your steps to bus stop 1473 next to the main entrance to the park. From here, bus nos. 25, 26, 66, 66a, 66b or 67 take you back to the city centre.**

06:30pm Get off the bus at bus stop 315 (Bachelors Walk/Liffey Street) and walk the few paces back, past Lower Liffey Street, and enter ⑫ **The Winding Stair →** p. 58 for an evening meal that you are not likely to forget in a hurry. The name comes from a poem by Nobel Prize winner William Butler Yeats, the beer from microbreweries and the food – with a distinctly Irish flavour to it – is cheaper at this time (pre-theatre menu 5.30pm–8.15pm) than later in the evening.

08:15pm Shortly after eight you will have had to vacate your table. Now it is time for a black beer and some traditional Irish music at **⑬ The Cobblestone** → p. 73 on Smithfield Square, Dublin's largest cobbled square, which you can reach by riding two stations with the Luas tram. If you are still fit after all that, **head off again in the direction of the Liffey, turn left along the northern bank and cross the Halfpenny Bridge into the ⑭ Temple Bar** → p. 34 district. Here, you can continue your tour until late into the night, trying out some of the pubs and bars.

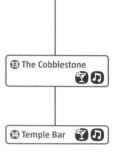

⑬ The Cobblestone

⑭ Temple Bar

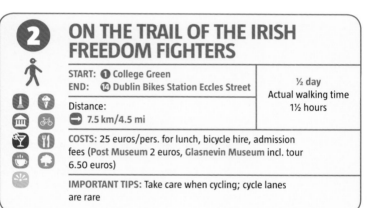

② ON THE TRAIL OF THE IRISH FREEDOM FIGHTERS

START: ① College Green END: ⑭ Dublin Bikes Station Eccles Street	½ day Actual walking time 1½ hours
Distance: ➡ 7.5 km/4.5 mi	
COSTS: 25 euros/pers. for lunch, bicycle hire, admission fees (Post Museum 2 euros, Glasnevin Museum incl. tour 6.50 euros)	
IMPORTANT TIPS: Take care when cycling; cycle lanes are rare	

Ireland's independence is not a topic that can be overlooked in Dublin. From the nationalists' perspective, the issue of an independent state was only partly resolved in 1921 because the six counties of Northern Ireland are still part of the United Kingdom. There are numerous museums and monuments throughout the city that commemorate the events of the Easter Rising of 1916 and other important dates. This walk guides you through Ireland's road to independence.

09:00am In the middle of the street on **① College Green** is a **statue of Henry Grattan**, who successfully campaigned for the independence of the Irish Parliament from the London government in 1782. His right arm held aloft, he looks out onto **② Trinity College** → p. 36, the training grounds for the Protestant regime that ruled over the Catholic majority in Ireland. **Go across to see it before wandering on to the parliament building to the left of Grattan, which**

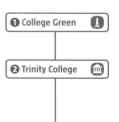

① College Green

② Trinity College

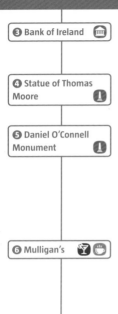

❸ Bank of Ireland 🏛

❹ Statue of Thomas Moore 🛈

❺ Daniel O'Connell Monument 🛈

❻ Mulligan's 🍸☕

is now home to the **❸ Bank of Ireland** → p. 35. Legislative independence then survived less than 20 years. After the rebellion of 1798 came the renewed incorporation of the Irish into the British parliament. **Cross at the traffic lights on Westmoreland Street and pass the ❹ statue of Thomas Moore** (1779–1852), whom the Irish celebrate as their national poet, **then go left towards O'Connell Bridge. On the north side of the bridge you'll immediately notice the impressive ❺ Daniel O'Connell Monument**. Daniel O'Connell (1775–1847), considered by his compatriots to be their liberator, instigated Catholic Emancipation. In 1841 he became the first Catholic mayor of Dublin. The four-winged female figures around his statue represent Ireland's provinces. One of them has a bullet hole in the chest from the 1916 Easter Rising. **Stay south of the Liffey and at Rosie Hackett Bridge, turn right into Hawkins Street and then left into Poolbeg Street. After the intersection with Corn Exchange Place you'll come across ❻ Mulligan's** → p. 75, one of Ireland's oldest pubs, on the left. As a young man, John F. Kennedy used to come here during the period he spent in Dublin working as a journalist, and James Joyce mentions Mulligan's in one of his short stories. The pub is famous for its Guinness, but if you feel it's still too early for a pint, you can stop off here anyway and have a cup of tea or coffee. **When you leave the pub, go to your left and turn left immediately into Tara Street. Cross over Butt Bridge in front of you and go to the right and across the street.** Behind the railway bridge, you have a wonderful view of

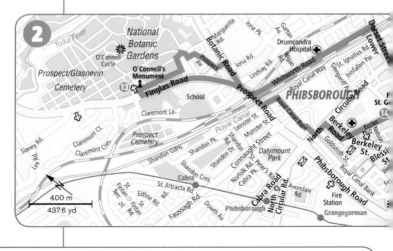

the **⑦ Custom House**. In 1921, rebels set fire to the building, which housed parts of the British administration, and burnt it down. **Go back under the railway bridge, cross over the riverside street and continue a few steps as far as the ⑧ statue of James Connolly.** Connolly was commander-in-chief of the 1916 rebellion and was seriously wounded during the occupation of the General Post Office (GPO). He was executed in Kilmainham Gaol. **Cross over Beresford Place to reach Abbey Street and on to the Abbey Theatre.** Opposite the building, three **⑨ bronze heads** mounted on short columns mark the spot where the Irish national flag was unveiled for the very first time in 1848. In the tricolour, the colour green stands for Ireland, orange for the royalist protestant Orangemen and white for the hope for reconciliation between the two sides.

Sculptures on Custom House

⑦ Custom House	🏛
⑧ Statue of James Connolly	👤
⑨ Bronze heads	🏛
⑩ Gelato di Natura	🍦

11:00am Now turn now right into O'Connell Street. After a few minutes you will be standing on the right-hand side of the street immediately after Earl Street N. in front of the best ice-cream parlour in Dublin: **⑩ Gelato di Natura** → p. 55. Take a short break with a dark chocolate ice

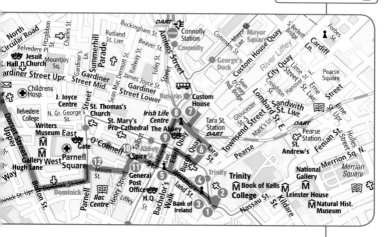

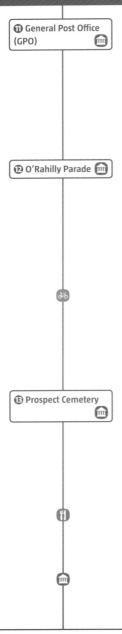

⑪ General Post Office (GPO) 🏛

⑫ O'Rahilly Parade 🏛

⑬ Prospect Cemetery 🏛

🚲

🍴

🏛

cream cone. Diagonally opposite stands the **⑪ General Post Office (GPO)** → p. 44, headquarters of the 1916 rebels. Pay a visit to the small **museum** which showcases not only the history of the postal service, but also the Easter Rising. On Easter Monday in 1916, a small group barricaded itself in the GPO and held out there for four days under artillery fire and in the burning ruins of the building. The survivors fled along **Henry Street (turn left at the GPO) and Moore Street (right). The lane to the right at the northern end of Moore Street, shortly before the spot where the rebels capitulated, is called ⑫ O'Rahilly Parade**. A plaque on the wall commemorates the rebel Michael O'Rahilly, citing the final letter he wrote, mortally wounded, to his wife: 'It was a good fight anyhow. Goodbye, darling'. From a military perspective, the rebellion of 1916 was of little significance, but the severity of the ensuing retaliatory measures turned the rebels into martyrs, the GPO into the nation's shrine and the fight for independence into a movement with broad support among the population. **Walk along Moore Street to the end and turn left into Parnell Street.** Get yourself a bicycle from **Dublin Bikes** → p. 112 and ride up **Dominick Street. At the next set of traffic lights, the route takes you right into Dorset Street,** which you then follow for 1.5 km (just under 1 mile). **Once you have crossed the Royal Canal, turn left into Whitworth Road, follow it to the end and then turn right into Prospect Avenue. Where the road forks, keep to the left** and after 250 m/ 275 yd you will reach the main entrance of **⑬ Prospect Cemetery** → p. 49, Ireland's largest burial ground. You'll see the round tower, the grave of Daniel O'Connel, from afar as you approach. Buy a map of the cemetery and make your way to each of the graves of the famous people who played key roles in Ireland's struggle for independence (Michael Collins, Brendan Behan, Eamon de Valera, Charles Stewart Parnell).

01:00pm The **INSIDER TIP Tower Café** (daily 10am–5pm | in the museum building) behind the cemetery book shop is a good choice for your lunch break. The coffee is sourced from organic cultivation and fair trade suppliers. You can get a value-for-money Irish breakfast until midday, and then lunch is served until 3pm. Finally, stop off at the **Glasnevin Museum** → p. 49 where you can learn all about Irish funerary cult in the interactive section in the basement. Incidentally, the cemetery is adjacent to the National Botanic Garden to the northeast, which you could also make a detour to. When you've seen enough, **leave the cemetery and the freedom fighters through the Prospect Gate exit on the eastern edge and cycle back to the nearest ⑭ Dublin Bikes Station Eccles Street**, to return your bicycle.

⑭ Dublin Bikes Station Eccles Street

---

❸ A CAPITAL IN ITS INFANCY

START: ❶ St Patrick's Park
END: ⑫ Brother Hubbard

½ day
Actual walking time
1 hour

Distance:
➡ 5 km/3.11 mi

COSTS: 35 euros/pers. food, admission fee
(❼ Guinness Storehouse 18 euros)

Over the centuries, the heart of Dublin has wandered continuously further east. This walk takes you back to the capital's origins, passing through The Liberties, where life follows a different rhythm than in the chic city centre, and ends in Capel Street, an often underrated, up-and-coming thoroughfare.

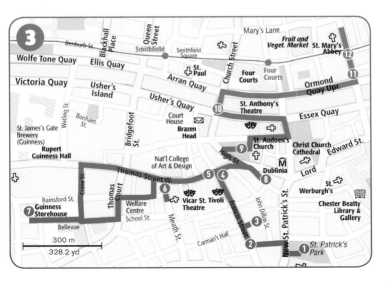

A trip to beer land: find out all about the typical black brew at the Guiness Storehouse

❶ St Patrick's Park

❷ Francis Street

❸ Church of St Nicholas

❹ Caffé Noto

10:00am The tour begins at ❶ **St Patrick's Park**, where green lawns and flower beds form a pretty framework for the view of the **Cathedral → p. 41**. At a well in the south-west corner of the park, Irish Patron Saint Patrick is said to have converted and baptised people in the Christian faith in the mid-5th century. The cathedral was founded on an island in the now subterranean river Poddle, whose dark waters formed a 'black pool', in Gaelic *dubh-linn,* which gave the city its name. Take a look inside the cathedral, where satirist and dean Jonathan Swift is buried, **before crossing Patrick Street and passing along Hanover Lane** to get to ❷ **Francis Street** with its selection of antiques dealers. Here, enticing shops selling ceramics, clocks and much more await you, **but the route takes you further to the right towards the north.** On the right, you will see the ❸ **Church of St Nicholas**, which was completed in 1832 and could only be built in the first place after the repeal of anti-Catholic legislation. A little further on stands the decorated brickwork of the Iveagh Market, constructed in 1907 and due to be fully rennovated in the style of London's Covent Garden in the coming years. The Tivoli Theatre stands opposite.

11:00am On the corner of Cornmarket there's good coffee to be had at ❹ **Caffé Noto**. The café is very spacious and boasts high ceilings. Instead of a pre-packed sandwich, you should order a brownie and a large Americano to go with it. This district, **The Liberties** → p. 47, is in a state of flux. The small shops on ❺ **Thomas Street** and ❻ **Meath Street** cater for people on modest incomes. Students from the nearby College of Art and Design lend a creative air to the district, and the influence of immigrants from Eastern Europe is also noticeable. Pop in for a look at the **NCBI Shop** *(73 Thomas Street)*, a second-hand shop run by the National Council for the Blind of Ireland. There's anything from clothing and books and CDs to household goods and other oddities – all at reasonable prices. **Take a detour to the left to the fake rock grotto behind St Catherine's Church on Meath Street** and to the colourful, over-the-top interior of the **Augustinian Church** → p. 48 **on Thomas Street** and experience how popular religious piety is expressed.

12:00pm Now you are getting close to the Guinness Brewery. **Carry on for a bit, then turn left into Crane Street. At the end of the road, turn right into Market Street and you will find yourself standing in front of the ❼ Guinness Storehouse** → p. 49, where you can get an insight into the history of the brewery and hear some interesting facts, too. At the end of the tour, you will of course be treated to a sample. **Return to the Cornmarket and continue eastwards. On the right, on the corner with Lamb Alley, you can see a surviving remnant of the medieval city wall. In the next alleyway on the right, Back Lane, after 100 m/110 yd on the left is ❽** Taylor's Hall, a charming brick building from 1706. The guildhall of the tailors is a rare relic of the former craftsmen's district. **Cross the road at the traffic lights. The line of streets – Cornmarket and High Street reaching eastward as far as Dame Street – marks the elevation upon which the Vikings founded a trading settlement in the 10th century. The route takes you between high stone walls down to the city gate dating back to 1275, ❾ St Audoen's Gate,** and the preserved 100-m/110-yd stretch of city wall. **Follow Cook Street to the right and turn left into Winetavern Street.** The office block which houses the municipal authorities on the right-hand side was constructed on the site of the former Viking settlement – despite a high-court ruling aimed at preventing this. Before building work began, archaeologists salvaged a host of everyday Viking artefacts – household items, tools, combs, coins – which today are today on display at the National Museum → p. 32.

❺ Thomas Street

❻ Meath Street

❼ Guinness Storehouse

❽ Taylor's Hall

❾ St Audoen's Gate

⑩ Father Matthew Bridge 🏛

⑪ Capel Street 👜 🍴 ☕

⑫ Brother Hubbard 🍴

01:00pm Go left along Merchants Quay as far as ⑩ **Father Matthew Bridge**, which you then cross. The priest after whom the bridge was named preached abstinence in the 19th century. On the other side you can see the **Four Courts** with the striking green dome which still stands as a symbol for any legal case despite the fact that the seat of the criminal court has been in Phoenix Park for some years now. **Walk past the court building, along Inns Quay and Ormond Quay up to Grattan Bridge, where you turn left into** ⑪ INSIDER TIP **Capel Street**. Underestimated by Dubliners and tourists alike, this street has still not not been completely modernised and offers a broad variety of shops: some sell new clothes and second-hand fashions, a computer store and a pet shop, everything from chic to shabby. There's even a branch (No. 39) of fashion designer **Louis Copeland**. The **Model Shop** (No. 13) is a paradise for boys of all ages – even grown-up ones. It has everything related to model making, and even if you don't want to buy anything it's worth a visit as the owner loves to start up a conversation and is positively bursting with enthusiasm. Capel Street also dishes up some fine options for your palate and your entertainment; there are restaurants for all budgets, pubs and bars. Explore these another time, though, as it's now time to treat yourself to lunch at ⑫ **Brother Hubbard** → p. 59. You won't regret it: salads and soups are homemade, taste delicious and are the perfect way to round off your tour.

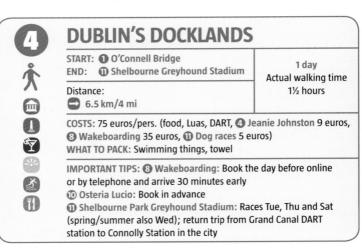

DUBLIN'S DOCKLANDS

4

START: ❶ O'Connell Bridge END: ⑪ Shelbourne Greyhound Stadium	1 day Actual walking time 1½ hours
Distance: ➡ 6.5 km/4 mi	

COSTS: 75 euros/pers. (food, Luas, DART, ❹ **Jeanie Johnston** 9 euros, ❽ **Wakeboarding** 35 euros, ⑪ **Dog races** 5 euros)
WHAT TO PACK: Swimming things, towel

IMPORTANT TIPS: ❽ **Wakeboarding:** Book the day before online or by telephone and arrive 30 minutes early
⑩ **Osteria Lucio:** Book in advance
⑪ **Shelbourne Park Greyhound Stadium:** Races Tue, Thu and Sat (spring/summer also Wed); return trip from Grand Canal DART station to Connolly Station in the city

A memorial to Ireland's Great Famine: the Famine Statues at the Custom House Quay

The Liffey divides Dublin into two unequal halves – the slightly shabbier north and the posher south. At the mouth of the river, in the old harbour district, a new, modern Dublin has emerged, where international companies have their European headquarters. The district is absolutely bursting with restaurants, pubs and entertainment offerings, but many elements of the Dublin of old and its history have also survived.

12:00pm Starting at ❶ O'Connell Bridge → p. 26 **go along the northern bank of the Liffey towards the harbour**, past **Custom House** and the International Financial Service Centre (IFSC), the symbol of Ireland's rise and fall. On the riverbank in front of these, it's worth taking a closer look at the ❷ **Famine Statues** → p. 47 and the ❸ **World Poverty Stone**, laid down to commemorate the United Nations International Day for the Eradication of World Poverty. The sculptures hark back to the great famine of the mid-19th century and the millions of Irish people who fled overseas to escape hunger – for example on the Jeanie Johnston. A faithful replica of the ❹ **Jeanie Johnston** including a

❶ O'Connell Bridge

❷ Famine Statues

❸ World Poverty Stone

❹ Jeanie Johnston

Famine Museum lies at anchor a little further on. The life-size figures under deck are meant to resemble passengers of the time.

01:30pm After the tour, continue on your way and shortly afterwards turn left into Excise Walk. At the end, after 250 m (275 yd), get on the Luas tram at Mayor Square in the direction of The Point and travel two stops to the terminus. Now you are in **Point Village** → p. 47, a new district for which ambitious plans were made that then had to be scaled down in the course of the financial crisis. The large underground car park, a cinema and ⑤ **The Gibson Hotel** → p. 80 – visible on the left – were completed. It's time for a break and the best place for you to take one is the heated terrace of this ultra-modern hotel. From there you'll have a great view over the harbour area. Try a cocktail – there are eight different types of gin alone! **Retrace your steps a short way on Upper Mayor Street and turn left into Castleforbes Road, which you follow as far as the Liffey. Here, turn right along North Wall Quay, past the architecturally noteworthy Convention Centre** → p. 47, **and left under the daringly constructed ⑥ Samuel Beckett Bridge** → p. 47. **At the end of the bridge, turn left and then right immediately into Cardiff Lane. Behind the post office turn left into Misery Hill,** which was named

⑤ The Gibson Hotel

⑥ Samuel Beckett Bridge

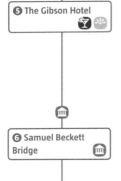

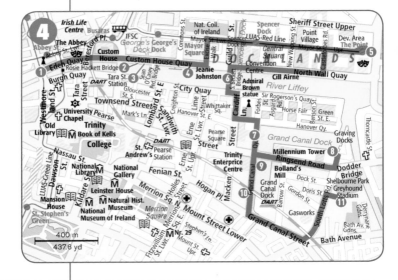

in remembrance of a lepra hospice which used to stand here. You now arrive at **❼ Grand Canal Square** with the **Bord Gáis Energy Theatre** → p. 77, which was designed by Daniel Libeskind. The square itself was the brainchild of American architect Martha Schwartz and features a kind of 'red carpet' interspersed with illuminated rods reaching down to the dock and crossed by a 'green carpet' of grass and vegetation.

❼ Grand Canal Square

02:30pm **Walk along Grand Canal Quay, turn left into Pearse Street, then left again into South Dock Road, which you follow down to the water.** This is where you'll be given the necessary equipment for **❽ INSIDER TIP wakeboarding** *(35 euros/15 mins., 60 euros/30-min lesson, including everything you need: helmet, neoprene suit and wakeboard | tel. 01 6 64 38 83 | www.wakedock.ie)*. It's a kind of water-skiing without a boat. Instead, you are towed backwards and forwards on a cable between two towers. Don't panic: if you do fall in the water, the operator is able to drive the handle back to you so you can pull yourself upright again. **Once you've dried off again after this refreshing interlude, it's back to Grand Canal Quay, which you follow down to the left until you see the floating ❾ Waterways Ireland Visitor Centre** → p. 30. Here, you can watch how to steer a barge or take part in a quiz on the subject of Ireland's waterways.

❽ Wakeboarding

❾ Waterways Ireland Visitor Centre

05:00pm You have probably worked up quite an appetite after all that wakeboarding. **Carry on along Grand Canal Quay to where it becomes Clanwilliam Terrace and to the Italian restaurant ❿ Osteria Lucio** *(daily. | tel. 01 6 62 41 99 | osterialucio.com | Moderate)*. As a starter, try the olives toasted over a wood fire, served with orange, fennel and rosemary and, as your main course, go for a pizza from the wood-burning stove topped with ham matured for 20 months, mozzarella and two-year-old Parmesan. In fine weather, you can dine outside. **After your meal, continue down Clanwilliam Terrace, turn left into Grand Canal Street and left again into St Lotts Road. Shortly before the end of the road you reach the ⓫ Shelbourne Park Greyhound Stadium** on the right, which is located in the park of the same name. Here, you can spend the evening watching the greyhound races and, if you're lucky, as the crowning moment of your tour, you could even collect your winnings from the bookmaker's.

❿ Osteria Lucio

⓫ Shelbourne Park Greyhound Stadium

TRAVEL WITH KIDS

The Irish may be fond of children but their capital is expensive for families and not ideal for children. The city centre has throngs of people, busy roads and dangerous traffic.

Nevertheless, Dublin does have a lot to offer children. Parks – like Merrion Square, St Stephen's Green and the large Phoenix Park – all have rolling lawns ideal for children to romp around on. And there is also a playground on the east side of St Stephen's Green.

The streets of Temple Bar offer excitement for all age groups. At No. 11a Eustace Street there's the children's cultural centre INSIDER**TIP** *The Ark (www. ark.ie)* with a colourful programme for children from 2–12 years of age, and in Grafton Street hilarious street artists perform to earn a living, and there are a number of bus tours.

Have the children had enough of the hustle and bustle of the city? High time for a trip to the seaside. In *Malahide* (125 E3) *(Ø O)* there is a sandy beach, in *Killiney* (125 F5) *(Ø O)* (p. 51) a nice pebble beach with a view over the Wicklow Mountains. Both are quick to get to with the DART from Dublin's centre.

INSIDER**TIP** **AIRFIELD FARM & GARDENS** (125 E3) *(Ø O)*
Cows and chickens, a garden with greenhouses (which supply the restaurant on the grounds) and a wooded park – you'll find all this and more on the farm. If all that's a bit too much nature, take a look in the garage: where else could you marvel at a Rolls Royce from 1927? There's a playground and numerous workshops too. *Sep–May daily 9.30am–5pm, June Mon–Fri 9.30am–5pm, Sat/Sun 9.30am–7pm, July–Aug daily 9.30am–7pm | admission fee 10, families 24 euros | Overend Way | Dundrum | tel. 019696666 | airfield.ie | bus 11, 14, 14C, 44, 44B, 75, 116 Balally | Luas Balally*

AQUARIUM NATIONAL SEA LIFE CENTRE (125 F6) *(Ø O)*
Right on the coastal promenade in the small town of *Bray* it's worth taking a look at the aquarium with its sharks, piranhas, seahorses and many other creatures. Easy to reach with the DART train. *Jan–March/Nov–Dec Mon–Fri 11am–5pm, Sat/Sun 10am–6pm, April–Oct daily 10am–5pm, Sat/Sun 10am–6pm | adults 12.50, children 9.50, online 8.50 and*

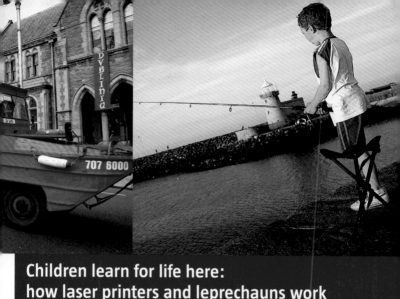

Children learn for life here: how laser printers and leprechauns work and what a real classic car looks like

7.50 euros respectively | www.visitsealife.com | DART Bray | then 5 min on foot

INSIDER TIP ▶ NATIONAL LEPRECHAUN MUSEUM ● (116 C3) (*ω F4*)

The leprechaun is a fairy tale creature – a tiny cobbler who knows where great treasures of gold are hidden. There are countless stories about them being caught by humans so that they would tell them the secret hiding place. The museum is dedicated to this mythical Irish creature with twelve interactive chapters. *Daily 9.30am–6.30pm, Sun 10.30am–6.30pm | adults 14, children under 17 years 10, family ticket 40 euros | 1 Jervis Street | www.leprechaunmuseum.ie | Luas Jervis Street*

SCIENCE GALLERY (117 F4) (*ω G5*)

You're travelling with curious children? Then take them to the Science Gallery. Combining science and art sounds quite adventurous to start with. But it works. For example at 'Sound Check', which explains what loudspeakers, laser printers and piccolos have in common. The gallery doesn't have a permanent exhibition, so there is always something new to see. Or sometimes nothing at all. Check the website first. *Tue–Fri 12pm–8pm, Sat/Sun 12pm–6pm | free admission | The Naughton Institute | Pearse Street | dublin.sciencegallery.com | DART, bus Pearse Street Station*

VIKING SPLASH (117 D6) (*ω G5*)

In and out of the water: unusual city tour in fantastic, old amphibious vehicles. Children under two aren't permitted to ride, older children must be accompanied by an adult. *Feb–Nov daily up to 7 trips from 10am to 4pm | adults 20, teens (13–17 years) 17, families 65 euros, July/Aug. 70 euros | from St Stephen's Green | tel. 01 70 76 00 00 | www.vikingsplash.ie | bus St Stephen's Green*

FESTIVALS & EVENTS

EVENTS

END JANUARY

Tradfest: A festival celebrating traditional music and folk at some unusual venues in Temple Bar. *www.templebartrad.com*

FEBRUARY

Dublin International Film Festival: A week filled with lots of Irish and international films. *Tel. 01 662 42 60 | www.dubliniff.com*

MARCH

⭐ *St Patrick's Day:* Five days of carnival atmosphere with fairs, markets, music and dance with a massive parade in the city on the 17th. *www.stpatricksday.ie*

APRIL

Messiah – 13 April: Open air performance of George Frideric Handel's oratorio on Fishamble Street

MAY

Africa Day – 25 May: Music, food and happenings – all about African culture. *www.africaday.ie*

JUNE

⭐ *Bloomsday – 16 June*: This is the day in 1904 that James Joyce's fiction 'Ulysses' unfolds. Guided walks and events at the locations all pay homage to the work. Information: *The James Joyce Centre (tel. 01 8 78 85 47 | www.jamesjoyce.ie)*

Dublin Writers Festival: Readings and presentations of famous international authors. *Mid-June | tel. 01 2 22 54 55 | www.dublinwritersfestival.com*

JUNE–AUGUST

Summer in Dublin: Open air events including free midday concerts at Merrion Square and in other parks and more. *End June–mid-Aug | www.dublincity.ie*

AUGUST

Dublin Horse Show: On the grounds of the Royal Dublin Society (RDS) in the suburb of Ballsbridge. INSIDER TIP *Ladies' Day (Wed–Sat of the 1st week in Aug | tickets tel. 08 1 83 00 20 74 | www.dublinhorseshow.com)* is a social event, where you wear extravagant hats, and there is also a large market fair that takes place around the main race track.

Everything goes green for St Patrick's Day but Dubliners celebrate more than their saint: beautiful horses, tough sports and literature

SEPTEMBER

Liffey Swim: Since 1920 participants have swum the Liffey 2.5 km/1.6 mi downstream to a festival at Custom House.

Dublin Fringe Festival: Theatre, dance, comedy and varied cabaret are proof of the inexhaustible creativity of the Irish. *Two weeks mid-Sept | tel. 01 8 17 16 77 | www.fringefest.com*

● **Culture Night:** The big night of free culture – from A to Z, in the entire urban area. *www.culturenight.ie*

OCTOBER

Dublin Theatre Festival: International theatre groups take to the city's stages. *End Sept–mid-Oct | www.dublintheatre festival.com*

Bram Stoker Festival: At the end of October Dubliners celebrate the author Bram Stoker ('Dracula') including an open-air opera, 'The Vampire', macabre city tours, readings and creepy-sounding 'Goth Karaoke'. *www.bramstokerfestival.com*

Dublin Marathon: Top class international athletes take part. *Last Mon in Oct | www.dublincitymarathon.ie*

NATIONAL HOLIDAYS

1 January	New Year
17 March	St Patrick's Day (National Day)
March/April	Easter Monday; Good Friday is not an official public holiday, but the pubs are closed.
1st Mon in May, June, Aug and last Mon in Oct	Bank Holiday
25/26 Dec	Christmas

LINKS, BLOGS, APPS & MORE

LINKS & BLOGS

www.visit-templebar.ie Temple Bar Traders site includes all sorts of listings about events, markets, exhibitions, pubs and where to find the craic!

www.storymap.ie Click on some of the speech bubbles on the city map and listen to the story. Locals like Seosamh O'Maolala (who tells a story about a monster that gets up to mischief at the Royal Canal) or the actress Maureen Grant (who speaks about her wild times at the Olympia Theatre, where she went on a ghost hunt with Laurel and Hardy and cuddled with Kris Kristofferson). Most of the speech bubbles you can click on are situated in the south of the city

www.spottedbylocals.com/dublin Which sandwich does Jess willingly queue up for? Which plays at the Gaiety Theatre can Barry recommend? Locals provide tips you won't find in travel guides – hidden parks, insider café, unusual statues, flea markets, special city walks. Much of it is unknown even to local Dubliners

www.philpankov.com The Russian photographer Philip Pankov studied photography in Dublin and is considered Ireland's best traditional photographer. He works with a Hasselblad 501CM and he prints out his pictures in his own dark room. See his website for some of his best black-and-white photos of Dublin

twitter.com/hashtag/dublinblog An excellent group blog – young writers and bloggers talk about life in Dublin and the goings-on with insight and humour

totallydublin.ie An informative resource about the cultural aspects of Dublin, especially with regard to films and music – also lots of videos. They promise to 'feature content on all facets of culture both Irish and international, music, film, fashion, bar and food reviews, and interviews'

www.lovindublin.com This website contains not only blogs on forthcoming events and news from in and around Dublin, but also offers tips on

Regardless of whether you are still researching your trip or already in Dublin: these addresses will provide you with more information, videos and apps to make your holiday even more enjoyable

special experiences, for example on the transformation of a tram into a restaurant for a day or a mobile café in a container

www.budgetplaces.com/dublin Here you will find dozens of videos about everyday life in the inner city, which give you an excellent idea of what to expect of Dublin. With lots of listings for inexpensive accommodation

www.visitdublin.com/see-do/talking-statues A special service from Dublin Tourism Office. Ten statues of famous people have a QR code attached to them, which you can scan with your smartphone. You will then get a call from James Joyce, Oscar Wilde, George Bernard Shaw or one of Dublin's other celebrities, who have interesting stories to tell.

www.nci.ie/ispy If you want to know what the weather is like in Dublin or if O'Shea's Pub is still open, have a look at this site with lots of live webcams in Dublin

Dublin Bus This app shows not only bus routes but also updated schedule times (GPS). Each bus stop has a number which you can enter in the app (iPhone and Android). You can then see immediately which bus is coming when

iGuide Dublin This is a mobile directory, each category leads you to various important sites or places of interest in your immediate environment. The app also shows you the 'offer of the day' – a cheap restaurant, a special discount at a boutique, etc. – and the latest news in Dublin

Walk Dublin With the aid of this free app from Dublin City Council you can safely set off to explore the city-centre streets on foot. Wherever you are, the app shows you 100 interesting spots close by – and it's interactive so you can add your own entries

Dublin for free Canny spenders can find information on free events in Dublin via this app

TRAVEL TIPS

ARRIVAL

🚢 There are a number of ferry options for travel from Britain to Ireland. *Irish Ferries (www.irishferries.com)* operate daily between Holyhead and Dublin Port. *P & O Ferries (www.POferries.com)* operate daily between Liverpool and Dublin Port or there is a fast service between Holyhead and Dublin Port with *Stena Lines (www.stenaline.ie)* with a choice of either a Fastcraft or a Superferry.

✈ Most national airlines offer regular direct flights to Dublin Airport *(www.dublinairport.com)*. Ireland's national carrier *Aer Lingus (www.aerlingus. com)* also has regular flights from Britain and North America and Ryanair *(www. ryanair.com)* always has discounted fares. The airlines regularly offer specials so it is worth checking with your travel agent for cheap packages. *Aircoach* buses *(www. aircoach.ie)* work around the clock, 6am–8pm every 10 min from the airport to the city. It takes about 40 minutes to get to the city centre on two routes, each via O'Connell Street to the suburbs of Sandyford and Leopardstown/Ballsbridge. Single 7 euros, return 12 euros. Attention: buses to the airport are often full at peak times. *Dublin Bus* is from 7am–11pm about every 10min, single 6 euros, return 10 euros, route 747 via O'Connell Street to the bus station (Busáras) (117 E2) *(ⓜ G4)*. The drive to Busáras takes about 30 min INSIDER TIP for a tight budget: route 41/41C to Lower Abbey Street, single 3,30 euros, about 45 min.

🚆 There is also a train-ferry connection from London to Dublin. Connections inside Ireland: arrival from the north Connolly Station, from the south and west Heuston Station west of the city centre.

CAR HIRE

Dublin has the same kind of traffic as any international city and if you decide to drive then you need to consider if you want to arrive in the city by car or if you want to rent one once there. Driving in Ireland is on the left-hand lane. The popular international car rentals are all at the airport. A local rental car company there is *Irish Car Rentals (tel. 06120 6040 | www.irishcarrentals.com)*. If you have a flat tyre: *Automobile Association (tel. 081822 7228)* or *RAC Motoring Service (tel. 18 00 80 54 98)*

CLIMATE, WHEN TO GO

Dublin has a temperate climate (due to the influence of the Gulf Stream) and is an all

RESPONSIBLE TRAVEL

It doesn't take a lot to be environmentally friendly whilst travelling. Don't just think about your carbon footprint whilst flying to and from your holiday destination but also about how you can protect nature and culture abroad. As a tourist it is especially important to respect nature, look out for local products, cycle instead of driving, save water and much more. If you would like to find out more about eco-tourism please visit: *www.ecotourism.org*

year round travel destination. Frost and snow seldom occur but it rains relatively consistently throughout the year. A good time to travel is March and April, when the weather is mild. The sunniest and driest months are May and June with seven hours of daily sunshine, but September and October can also be nice. The temperature rarely gets much higher than 20°C/68°F. Even in summer you should be prepared for cold fronts on a daily basis, with constantly changing weather, so it is best to always pack warm clothing and rain gear.

CONSULATES & EMBASSIES

AMERICAN EMBASSY (123 E4) *(ᗰ H6)*
42 Elgin Road | Ballsbridge | Dublin 4 | tel. +353 16 68 87 77 | ie.usembassy.gov

BRITISH EMBASSY (125 E5) *(ᗰ J7)*
29 Merrion Road | Ballsbridge | Dublin 4 | tel. +353 12 05 37 00 | britishembassyin ireland.fco.gov.uk/en

CUSTOMS

UK citizens do not have to pay any duty on goods brought from another EU country as long as tax was included in the price and they are for private consumption. The limits are: 800 cigarettes, 400 cigarillos, 200 cigars, 1kg smoking tobacco, 10L spirits, 20L liqueurs, 90L wine, 110L beer. Travellers from the USA, Canada, Australia or other non-EU countries are allowed to enter with the following tax-free amounts: 200 cigarettes or 100 cigarillos or 50 cigars or 250g smoking tobacco. 2L wine and spirits with less than 22vol % alcohol, 1L spirits with more than 22vol % alcohol content.

CURRENCY CONVERTER

£	€	€	£
1	1.11	1	0.90
3	3.33	3	2.70
5	5.55	5	4.50
13	14.45	13	11.70
40	44.45	40	36
75	83.33	75	67.50
120	133.50	120	108
250	278	250	225
500	611	500	450

$	€	€	$
1	0.88	1	1.14
3	2.64	3	3.41
5	4.40	5	5.70
13	11.43	13	14.80
40	35.20	40	45.50
75	66	75	85.30
120	105.50	120	136.50
250	220	250	285
500	440	500	569

For current exchange rates see www.xe.com

Travellers to the US who are residents of the country do not have to pay duty on articles purchased overseas up to the value of $800, but there are limits on the amount of alcoholic beverages and tobacco products. For the regulations for international travel for US residents please see *www.cbp.gov*.

DUBLIN PASS

The *Dublin Pass* gives you free access to about 30 places of interest, free airport transfer with the Aircoach as well as various specials. You can get the pass online (www.dublinpass.ie) and in the *Dublin Tourism* offices, 52 euros for one, 73 for two, 83 for three and 104 for five days. Many attractions like the National Museum are free of charge anyway – it is INSIDER TIP worth it only for visitors that go to many sites.

ELECTRICITY

Voltage: 230 Volt. Irish electrical sockets are designed for three-pin plugs.

EMERGENCY SERVICES

Police (Garda) *(tel. 9 99 or 1 12)*. This number is also valid for rescue services, the fire department and coastguard services.

HEALTH

UK nationals and nationals with the European medical aid card (EHIC) can make use of the doctors and hospitals. The bill gets paid the same way as back home with the card. It is essential that citizens from all other countries take out private medical insurance. You don't need to look far to find a pharmacy in Dublin. There are numerous pharmacies and *Boots* outlets.

IMMIGRATION

Citizens of the UK, USA, Canada, Australia and New Zealand only need a valid passport to enter all countries of the EU. Children below the age of 12 need a children's passport.

INFORMATION

TOURISM IRELAND UK
103 Wigmore Street | London W1U 1QS | tel. +44 20 75 18 08 00 | www.discover ireland.com/gb

TOURISM IRELAND USA
345 Park Avenue | New York, NY 10154 | tel. +1 212 418 08 00 | www.discover ire land.com/us

DUBLIN TOURISM CENTRE
The tourism centre has several branches in the city: *Airport Dublin* (125 E4) *(ΩΩ 0) (arrivals | daily 8am–10pm); main office: St Andrew's Church* (117 D4) *(ΩΩ G5) (25 Suffolk Street | Mon–Sat 9am–5.30pm, Sun 10.30am–3pm); north of the Liffey: 14 O'Connell Street Upper* (120 C5) *(ΩΩ G4) (Mon–Sat 9am–5pm | tel. 353 18 50 23 03 30 (*))*

MONEY & CREDIT CARDS

The currency is the euro. ATMs for EC cards are available on almost every street corner in the city centre. The banks open Mon–Fri 10am–4pm, Thu until 5pm, and certain branches also open on Saturdays. Almost all credit cards are accepted in most of the shops, hotels and restaurants. However, some private bed and breakfast establishments prefer to be paid in cash. Best ask when checking in!

NEWSPAPERS

The most important daily newspapers in Dublin are the serious, liberal-minded *Irish Times,* the lighter, slightly more conservative *Irish Independent* and the *Examiner.* The *Evening Herald* is an evening paper. You can also get English newspapers at most stores, some of which with Irish editions.

OPENING HOURS

Business hours are generally Mon–Sat 9am–6pm but some do vary their closing times and have longer hours in the evening. Many shops are also open on Sunday afternoons. In the city centre most of the shops don't close before 8pm on Thursdays.

PHONE & MOBILE PHONE

Using cell phones with GMS standard and roaming service in Ireland is hassle-free but can be expensive if you don't have an EU SIM card. Since 2017 you can make calls within the EU without roaming charges if you have an EU SIM card. Avoid the few telephone boxes that are still standing because they are extremely expensive. Cheaper are calls from call shops, of which the city centre has many. You can get phone cards for 10, 15 and 20 euros at the post office. Telephone directory: *118 50*. The dialling code for Ireland is *+353* and the area code is *(01)* for Dublin.

POST

Dublin's post offices are open Mon–Fri 9.30am–6pm, the General Post Office on O'Connell Street (117 D2) (*M G4*) Mon–Sat 10am–5pm.

PUBLIC TRANSPORT

In Dublin's compact city centre many areas can be reached comfortably on foot. The train routes travel around the periphery of the city centre. There are numerous bus routes, but with the wide variety of different routes you need some help to get yourself orientated.

BUSES

Buses stop on request. 'An Lár' on the destination indicates a bus that will take you to the city centre. Especially handy among the different multiple journey tickets are the *Rambler Tickets*. They allow trips on all routes in the city district for 31.50 euros for five days. A combined bus–Luas-DART ticket (Leap Family Card) costs 10 euros per

BUDGETING

Guinness	£4–5.40/$4.10–6.80 *for a pint*
Coffee	£2.50/$2.80 *per cup*
Fish and chips	£8/$10.25 *for a portion*
Bus ticket	£1.80–3/$2.30–3.75 *for a single fare with up to 3 stops*
Theatre	from £27/$34 *per ticket*

day and is valid for two adults and four children. If you're staying longer, it's worth buying a rechargeable *Leap Card (deposit 5 euros, minimum balance 5 euros)*. Firstly, travel by bus, Luas and DART is cheaper and, secondly, you don't have to have the exact fare on you (drivers don't give change!). The ticket is available online (arrives by post) and in more than 500 outlets. You can top it up there too. Timetables and tickets: *Dublin Bus Office* (117 D2) (*M G4*) *(Mon–Sat 9am–5.30pm | 59 O'Connell Street Upper | tel. 01 8 73 42 22 | www.dublinbus.ie)*

DART

Dublin Area Rapid Transport (DART) is the rail line that connects the northern and southern suburbs and coastal regions with the inner city – Connolly Station north of the Liffey, Tara Street and Pearse Street in the south. For ● trips to the coast and for Dublin visitors with accommodation near the DART stations, it is really convenient *(every 10–15 min from 6am–midnight)*. The day ticket for 11.70 euros is worth it after four rides. For trips you best buy a return ticket at a vending machine or ticket counter. *www.irishrail.ie*

DUBLIN BIKES 🌳

Dublin is not the most bicycle-friendly city, the bicycle paths are not always separate but often consist of a brown line painted on to the street, and the car drivers are not very considerate. But bicycles are now also part of the public transport system as the city has adopted the practice of renting out bicycles. 450 robust bicycles are available at more than 100 stations in the city centre; the individual stations are at the most 300 m/ 330 yd apart from each other. In order to rent a bike, you have to become a member and for tourists it is worth getting the 3-day membership for 5 euros. You can pay at more than 30 stations with your credit card. The membership ID carries a PIN number which you will need when taking a bicycle. The first 30 min are free. Afterwards it costs 50c per hour, 1.50 for two hours, 3.50 for three hours and 6.50 for four hours and 2 euros for every following half hour. You can find information about the bike sharing scheme and the stations at *www.dublinbikes.ie*.

ECOCABS ● 🌳

Strong cyclists will take you to any destination within Dublin's city centre in modern, covered tricycles, also in a radius of about 2km/1.2mi around the O'Connell Bridge. They ride between 10am and 7pm and have certain stops, but can also be waved down. They are sponsored by companies, so you don't need to pay them, but a tip will be greatly appreciated. Don't mistake the Ecocabs with the rickshaws or bicycle taxis that demand a fee! *www.ecocabs.ie*

LUAS

The fast and modern commuter rail, Luas, rides on two routes. The red route takes

WEATHER IN DUBLIN

	Jan	Feb	March	April	May	June	July	Aug	Sept	Oct	Nov	Dec
Daytime temperatures in °C/°F	8/46	8/46	10/50	12/54	15/59	18/64	20/68	19/66	17/63	14/57	10/50	8/46
Nighttime temperatures in °C/°F	2/36	2/36	2/36	3/37	6/43	9/48	11/52	10/50	9/48	6/43	3/37	2/36
☀️	2	3	4	6	7	7	6	5	4	3	2	2
☂️	13	11	10	11	11	11	13	13	12	12	12	13
≈≈≈	9/48	8/46	7/45	8/46	9/48	11/52	13/55	14/57	14/57	13/55	12/54	10/50

☀️ Sunshine hours/day ☂️ Precipitation days/month ≈≈≈ Water temperature in °C/°F

you from 3 Arena and the Docklands parallel to the Liffey on the northern bank, crosses over the river to Heuston Station and then to the south-west suburbs. The green route connects the southern suburbs of Dublin with Cabra in the north of the city via the city centre, where you can connect with the red line *(every 10 min or more frequently from 5.30am–0.30am, Sat from 6.30am, Sun from 7am | www.luas.ie)*. You can get Luas-tickets at vending machines and in shops near the stops.

SIGHTSEEING TOURS

There are a number of good walking tours for the Dublin visitor. A favourite is the ● *Literary Pub Crawl (April–Oct daily, Nov–March Thu–Sat 7.30pm, starting at the pub The Duke | Duke Street | www.dublinpubcrawl.com | tel. 016 70 56 02)*. Two actors lead you through the pubs and entertain you with pieces by Samuel Beckett, Oscar Wilde and the like. With the brochure ● *Rock 'n' Stroll Trail (at the Tourist Office or free as iWalk with podcast to download from www.visitdublin.com)* music lovers will find where stars like U2 lived and worked. You can also view Dublin from the Liffey: boat trips from *Bachelors Walk (March–Nov four to six times daily about 45 min for 15, online 13.50 euros | tel. 014 73 40 82 | www.dublindiscovered.ie)* start on the north bank near Halfpenny Bridge. You can literally get a taste of Dublin: with the INSIDER TIP *Dublin Tasting Trail (55 euros | tel. 014 97 12 45 | www.fabfoodtrails.ie/dublin-tastingtrail)* which mixes sightseeing with culinary pleasures. The 2.5 hour tour takes you to markets, fish shops, bakeries, butcheries and cheese shops – some have been in one family for four to five generations. And best of all: at each one of the many stops you can have a taste. The tour starts at 10am on Fridays

and Saturdays depending on the route at the various points in the centre.

TAXI

You can easily catch a taxi even on weekends. There are taxi ranks in the city centre at College Green, at Aston Quay and on O'Connell Street. The basic fee is 3.60 euros during the day and 4 euros at night for the first 400 metres. Every following kilometre costs 1.10–1.75 euros depending on the distance. A ride from the airport to the city centre costs upwards of 30 euros. There are sufficient taxis, but when it is important to be on time (for example when going to the airport) you should order a taxi beforehand e.g.: *A to B Cabs (tel. 016 77 22 22)*, *Checkers Cabs (tel. 018 34 34 34)*, *Pony Cabs (tel. 016 61 22 33)* or via the international app *My Taxi*.

TIPPING

10–15 per cent on the price of the meal, without drinks, is the norm for a tip at a restaurant, but that is only if an amount has not already been added as a service charge; 10 per cent of the cost of the ride is a standard tip for a taxi driver. As a rule no tip is given in pubs if you fetch your drink at the bar, but if you are served at a table, you should tip.

TIME

The time in Ireland is Greenwich Mean Time (GMT).

WEIGHTS & MEASURES

The metric system is used in Ireland with one exception: draft beer in the pubs is in pints.

STREET ATLAS

The green line indicates the Discovery Tour 'Dublin at a glance'
The blue line indicates the other Discovery Tours

All tours are also marked on the pull-out map

Exploring Dublin

The map on the back cover shows how the area has been subdivided

Broadstone-DIT ●A

Temple Cottages
Mountjoy

Granby Row
The Children
of Lir ♦

Garber of Remembrance
Gate

Constitution
Temple St. Upper

Henrietta
Lane
Upper

2 V1

Granby
Lane

Parnell Sq. West

Rotunda
Hospital

N2
N

Prebend St.

King's
Inns

Henrietta
Convent
Henrietta St.

Dominican
Church

Dominick St.

Granby Pl.

Ambassador
Parnell Stat.

Hostel

Brunswick
St. North

Linenhall
Terrace

Coleraine St.

Linenhall Parade

Lisburn St.

Bolton St.

D.I.T.

King's Inns Ln.

Dominick St. Lower

Dominick La.

Dominick

O'Connell Uppe

Church St. Upper

Ann St. North

North King St.

Court
House

St.
Michan's
Park

Green St.

Britain St. Little

Ryder's
Row

Parnell St.

Lotus

The Parnell
Centre
Cineworld

Chapel Lane

Ilac
Centre

Sampson's
Lane

James

Ge
Post O
(G.

Stirrup
Lane

Ball's
Lane

Ann St. Lane

Betterson St.

Anglesea
Row

Wolfe
Tone

Jervis St.

Henry
St.

Proby's Lane

Nicholas
Avenue

Church
Terrace

Cuckoo Lane

George's Hill

Capel St. Upr.

The Church

Jervis
Centre

Hotel Yard

SMITH
FIELD

May Lane

R108

Mary's
Lane

Greek St.

St. Michan's

Little Mary St.

3

Mary St.

St. Mary's
Abbey M

LUAS-Red Line

Abbey St.

Jervis

Byrne's Lane

St.

Abbey St. Upper

Lot

1

St. Michan's
Church

Chancery St.

River Liffey
House

Dublin Corp.
Fruit and
Vegetable
Market

Mary's Abbey

Capel St.

Swift's
Row

St. Great

Bachelor's
Walk

Boat

3

Four Courts

Four Courts

Chancery Pl.

Charles St. West

Ormond
Square

Strand

St. Little

Strand

Ormond Quay Lower

Millenium
Bridge

Ha'penny
Bridge

Quay

Crampt

Inns Quay

Fr. Matthew Bridge

O'Donovan
Rossa Bridge

Ormond Quay Upper

River Liffey

Grattan
Bridge

N4

Wellington Quay

N4

Projects Art
Centre

Temple

15

Bar

Quay

12

Merchants Quay

Wood Quay

Essex Quay

Exchange St.
Lower

Parliament St.

Essex St. West

Crane La.

Eustace St.

Cecilia
St.

Crow St.

Cope St.

Central
Bank

Adam and Eve's
Church

1

3

Whitefriar St.

Civic
Offices

Copper Alley

Lord Edward St.

Olympia

Dame
St.

BAR

1

St. Audoen's
Church

Cook St.

Christ Church
Cathedral

Castle St.

City Hall

Dame St.

Dame Lane

Dame Lane

Andrews
Lane

4

Bridge St. Upr.

Lamb Alley

St. Audoen's

High St.

Dublinia M

Back Lane

Christchurch
Pl.

1

St. Werburgh's
Church

Dublin Castle

Fade
St.

Exchequer St.

George St. Castle
Arcade

Corn
Market

Taylor's
Hall

Ship St.
Little

Chester
Beatty
Library

Dubh
Linn Garden ★

South Great George's St.

Iveagh
Market

Dean Swift
Square

Ross Road

Werburgh St.

Ship St. Great Upper

4

Stephen St.

Stephen St. Lower

William St.

Tivoli
Theatre

THE
LIBERTIES

Swift's
Alley

Francis St.

Bride Road

Iveagh
Trust
Buildings

Chancery La.

Bull Alley St.

Golden Lane

Digges St. Lower

Aungier St.

King St.

Mercer St. Lower

St. Steph
Green Ce.

Glovers

Carman's Hall

Hanover Lane

St. Patrick's Park

Wood St.

Bride

Carmelite
Church

Mark's Alley
West

3

St. Patrick's
Cathedral

5

Whitefriar St.

York

Royal College
of Surgeons

St.

Alley

Dean St.

R110

St. Patrick's Close

Marsh's
Library

Peter St.

National
Archives

Peter Row

D.I.T.

Redmonds Hill

Aungier St.

Mercer St. Upper

Digges
St. Upr.

Cuffe Lane

LUAS-
Green Line

The Coombe
Relief St.

New Row South

Kevin St. Upper

Bishop St.

New

Bride St.

Kevin St. Lower

Cuffe St.

R110

6

150 m

164 yd

122

N 81

116

Cuffe St.

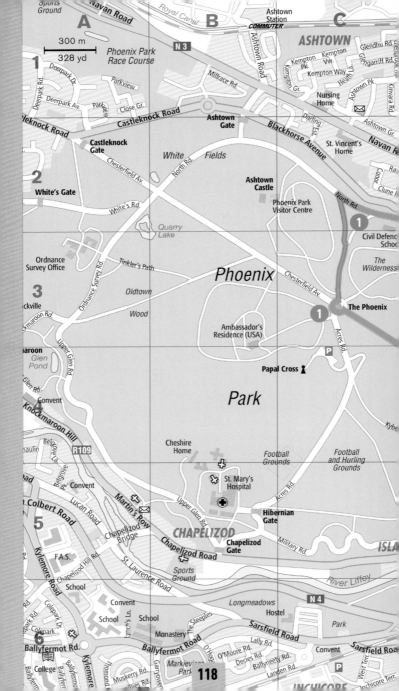

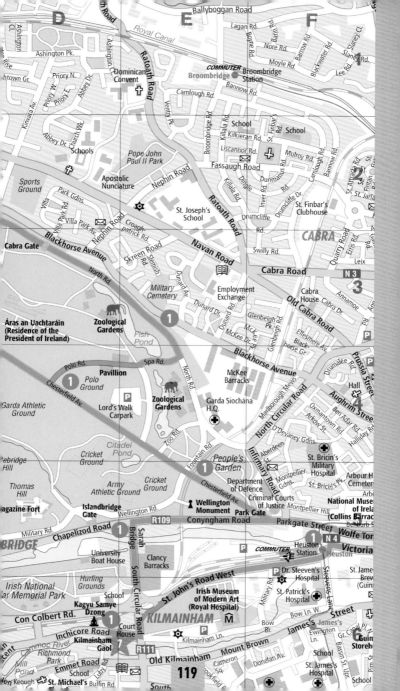

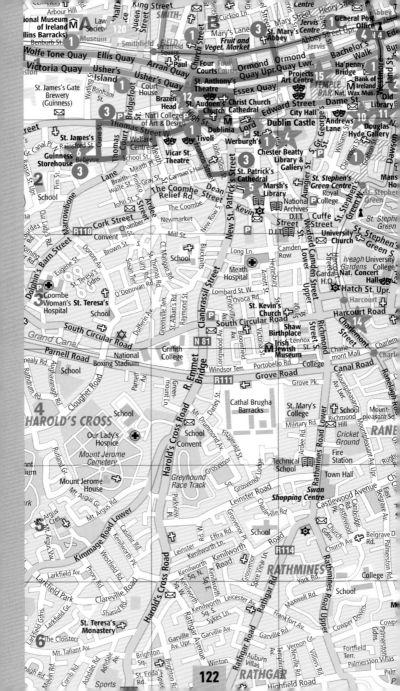

122

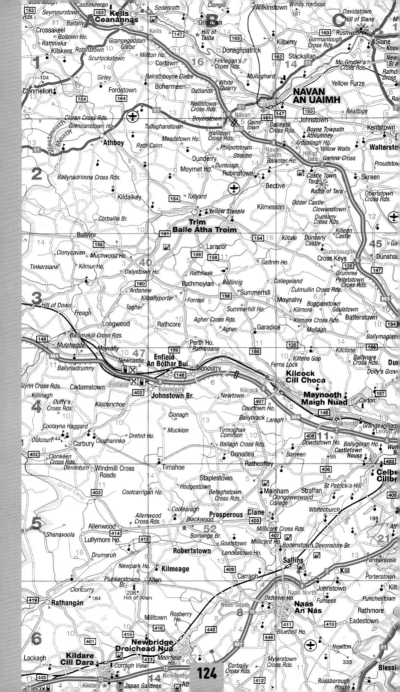

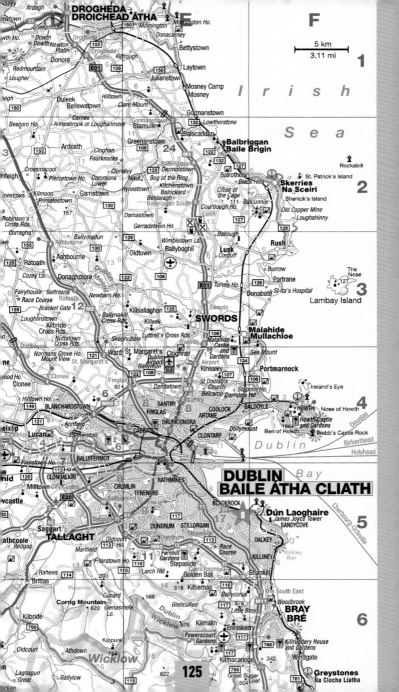

This index lists a selection of the streets and squares shown in the street atlas

STREET INDEX

KEY TO STREET ATLAS

M̂	Museum
🎭	Stage / Bühne
⌂	Information
✝	Church / Kirche
✡	Synagogue / Synagoge
⊕	Hospital / Krankenhaus
✪	Police / Polizei
✉	Post
📖	Library / Bibliothek
♟	Monument / Denkmal
❋	Botanic garden / Botanischer Garten
🐘	Zoo
P	Parking / Parkplatz
⛺	Youth Hostel / Jugendherberge
—●—	Tram with station / Tram mit Station
DART	Dublin Area Rapid Transit
◻	Remarkable building / Bemerkenswertes Gebäude
◻	Public building / Öffentliches Gebäude
◻	Green / Grünfläche
◻	Uncovered area / Unbebaute Fläche
▨▨▨	Pedestrian zone / Fußgängerzone
▬▬▬	MARCO POLO Discovery Tour 1 / MARCO POLO Erlebnistour 1
▬▮▬	MARCO POLO Discovery Tours / MARCO POLO Erlebnistouren
★	MARCO POLO Highlight

MARCO POLO TRAVEL GUIDES

Algarve
Amsterdam
Andalucia
Athens
Australia
Austria
Bali & Lombok
Bangkok
Barcelona
Berlin
Brazil
Bruges
Brussels
Budapest
Bulgaria
California
Cambodia
Canada East
Canada West / Rockies
& Vancouver
Cape Town &
Garden Route
Cape Verde
Channel Islands
Chicago & The Lakes
China
Cologne
Copenhagen
Corfu
Costa Blanca
& Valencia
Costa Brava
Costa del Sol &
Granada
Costa Rica
Crete
Cuba
Cyprus (North and
South)
Devon & Cornwall
Dresden
Dubai

Dublin
Dubrovnik &
Dalmatian Coast
Edinburgh
Egypt
Egypt Red Sea Resorts
Finland
Florence
Florida
French Atlantic Coast
French Riviera
(Nice, Cannes & Monaco)
Fuerteventura
Gran Canaria
Greece
Hamburg
Hong Kong & Macau
Ibiza
Iceland
India
India South
Ireland
Israel
Istanbul
Italy
Japan
Jordan
Kos
Krakow
Lake District
Lake Garda
Lanzarote
Las Vegas
Lisbon
London
Los Angeles
Madeira & Porto Santo
Madrid
Maldives
Mallorca
Malta & Gozo
Mauritius

Menorca
Milan
Montenegro
Morocco
Munich
Naples & Amalfi Coast
New York
New Zealand
Norway
Oslo
Oxford
Paris
Peru & Bolivia
Phuket
Portugal
Prague
Rhodes
Rome
Salzburg
San Francisco
Santorini
Sardinia
Scotland
Seychelles
Shanghai
Sicily
Singapore
South Africa
Sri Lanka
Stockholm
Switzerland
Tenerife
Thailand
Tokyo
Turkey
Turkey South Coast
Tuscany
United Arab Emirates
USA Southwest
(Las Vegas, Colorado,
New Mexico, Arizona
& Utah)
Venice
Vienna
Vietnam
Zakynthos & Ithaca,
Kefalonia, Lefkas

Travel with Insider Tips

INDEX

This index lists all sights, museums, and destinations, plus the names of important people and key words featured in this guide. Numbers in bold indicate a main entry.